DATE DUE

Betty's Summer Vacation

Works of Christopher Durang published by Grove Press

THE MARRIAGE OF BETTE AND BOO

LAUGHING WILD AND BABY WITH THE BATHWATER

CHRISTOPHER DURANG EXPLAINS IT ALL FOR YOU
   THE NATURE AND PURPOSE OF THE UNIVERSE
   'DENTITY CRISIS
   TITANIC
   THE ACTOR'S NIGHTMARE
   SISTER MARY IGNATIUS EXPLAINS IT ALL FOR YOU
   BEYOND THERAPY

BETTY'S SUMMER VACATION

CHRISTOPHER DURANG

Betty's Summer Vacation

Grove Press
New York

ISBN 0-7394-0794-5

To John Augustine and Kristine Nielsen

Foreword

For me, as both a citizen and a producer, *Betty's Summer Vacation* arrived on my desk in the nick of time. As a dyed-in-the-wool liberal humanist, I'd always assumed the proper response to our burgeoning junk culture was to sequester myself into a little ivory tower of civility. But lately the waves seemed to be turning tidal, rendering my little tower into a crumbling sand castle. Try as I might, whenever the latest scandal or horror hit, to duck into my office and close the door behind me, eventually the tabloid ooze would start seeping under my door and suck me into it. During late-night channel surfing, my guard would fall, and I'd pause to hear the talking heads and waggish stand-ups holding forth or cracking wise about whatever latest headline. By the time *The New York Times* would begin holding forth their in-depth news analyses and tsk-tsking Op-Ed-page sociological tomes, you would inevitably find me poring over them.

As a producer of new American plays who oversees the reading of twelve to fifteen hundred play submissions annually, I found the glut of misguided efforts to skewer or portray this state of affairs perhaps even more dispiriting. Hand me a play and tell me it's a hilarious satire on our tabloid culture and watch my eyes glaze over. The targets are too easy. The results usually seem shrill and rote. On the other hand, for me, the kind of theater that seeks to probe the dark underbelly of society with grim realism usually seems voyeuristic and sensationalistic. How can the violence of the world ever be real to us, especially when it gets translated into infotainment within minutes of its occurrence? *Betty's Summer Vacation,* however, follows a much different route through these poles of absurdity and horror. The first act follows an inverse dynamic from that created by tabloid events in real life where repugnance deteriorates rapidly into sick humor, beginning with a breezy nonchalance that curdles into revulsion. Act Two one-ups itself by shifting focus from the lurid contents of the world (which, by the way, have remained offstage and are therefore completely unreal to us anyway), to our reaction to and appetite for these events. Thus we essentially witness the tabloidization of the world. In the face of this inexorable, degrading force, Betty becomes the lone voice of reason, arguing sensibly and with increasing exasperation for the basic, humane tenets of civilization. But Betty might as well be *Alice in Wonderland* with Voices from the Ceiling playing the role of Red Queen.

The achievement of *Betty's Summer Vacation* seems even more satisfying when viewed in the context of Christopher's recent artistic history. Many would agree Durang's early career reached its apex with *The Marriage of Bette and Boo,* produced at the Public Theater in 1985. Few remember his next play, *Laughing Wild,* produced at Playwrights Horizons in 1987. This bravely personal and critically important transitional play, in which Chris also acted, costarring with E. Katherine Kerr, was roundly dismissed at the time, treated almost as if it wasn't a play at all. In retrospect, it seems ahead of its time, uncannily foreshadowing the deluge of performance artists of recent years. But it also marks a shift in his work more directly toward social satire. The targets of his earlier work were frequently the grotesqueries that imprint us in childhood, but with *Laughing Wild* his perspective seems more adult, in a way, focusing more on the skewed indignities we endure every day. Chris's output tapered off somewhat in the following decade, but he did wrestle again with these contemporary hobgoblins in *Media Amok,* produced at the American Repertory Theatre in 1992, and *Sex and Longing,* Chris's dark, ambitious mock epic, produced by Lincoln Center in 1996. While this production featured a game, Valkyrian performance by Sigourney Weaver and an exquisite comedic turn by Dana Ivey, it seemed to get swallowed up by the Cort Theatre, and even Chris himself admits it was over-written. Still, the torrent of incontinent critical vitriol it unleashed seems puzzling even now. One wondered if Chris would ever write again. In this light, *Betty's Summer Vacation* feels like a triumph. Undeterred by the fear and loathing elicited by the dark and thorny *Sex and Longing*, Chris seemed determined to take the darkness one step further. Yet he did so with a rigorous formal control that not only concentrated his themes, but also sharpened the detail and intimacy of his characterizations, and allowed the natural cheerful perversity of his voice to flourish. Chris had been after something as an artist for about twelve years. With *Betty's Summer Vacation*, he nailed it.

Of course, it's one thing to appreciate *Betty's Summer Vacation*, and quite another to produce it. It's easily one of the most outrageous plays I have ever read, and I knew it would also prove to be one of the trickiest to produce. The production would have to negotiate the same line between horror and absurdity that makes the play so successful. Push the humor and the play's darkness would cut your legs off. Push the darkness and you would suffocate in amorality. Again, *Alice in Wonderland* provides a useful paradigm for approaching the production: The world is morally upside down, but seems perfectly normal to its inhabitants. In this regard, Nicholas Martin proved an especially felicitous choice for director. He understood instinctively that the play requires actors who are quick, focused, direct, and charming, and we assembled a sublimely spirited ensemble headed by the indefatigable and inimitable Kristine Nielsen as Mrs. Siezmagraff and the droll, Keane-eyed killer screamer Kellie Overbey as Betty. The production was also immeasurably helped by its peerless design team, which included Kevin Adams's lights, Michael Krass's costumes, Kurt Kellenberger's sound, Peter Golub's pitch-perfect original music, and especially the extraordinary set by Tom Lynch, whose eight-doored ground plan pre-mapped the easy, high-energy fluidity of the stage movement, and whose collapsing ceiling and receding set wagon so effectively punctuated the play's climactic moments. Ultimately, of course, it was Nicky's direction that was responsible for the controlled energy and tone of the production. Very few premiere productions so fully realize the original potential and intent of their scripts.

I was certain, when we undertook *Betty's,* that the production would be controversial. Satire at its keenest always portrays that which it mocks, and I knew the representation of such vile and offensive behavior as cheerfully purveyed by the characters in *Betty's* would be sure to offend some. And it surely did. In fact, it seemed impossible not to have a powerful response to the play. Those who disliked it tended to *hate* it. Those who liked it tended to *love* it. But as we progressed through the preview period, where we made a few judicious but important edits, the tide of ratio seemed to swing heavily toward the latter camp. In the end, the play still got under the skin of some audience members. But when I would observe their indignation, I began to imagine them going home and resolutely putting on some Bach or sitting down with a little Dickens, striving to create a little secure humanist sanctuary for themselves, proving themselves ultimately to be kindred spirits with Betty. So really, the play had its desired effect after all.

Tim Sanford
Artistic Director
Playwrights Horizon
New York City
December 9, 1999

INTRODUCTION
Betty, Breathing, and the Bounds of Comedy

by Michael Feingold

Provocative in every imaginable way, *Betty's Summer Vacation* is never more so than in the questions it raises about what comedy is, and how far it's entitled to go. Rape, murder, and mutilation, accompanied by a laugh track? What world are we in? And how can it be one that we voluntarily choose to visit for amusement? This isn't the first play by Christopher Durang to have challenged and conquered such preconceptions. Images of horror have fueled his comedy from the very beginning; for him, laughter is the defiant assertion of life, in the face of a world that leads us toward death in increasingly terrifying ways. But in *Betty's Summer Vacation,* he finds new, and newly unsettling, ways to stage this confrontation, which may stir his audience into rephrasing their troubling old questions even as they roar with laughter. Other great comedies—and yes, I'll go so far as to call this a great comedy—may divide one segment of the audience from another; *Betty's Summer Vacation,* with its images of casual violence and the casual response they provoke, is likely to aggravate any division you find within yourself.

But that's okay. Comedy—in the classical, not the laugh-line, sense—exists to chastise and celebrate our flaws. It paints us as the horrible creatures we are, and then dares us to laugh at that. And indeed, [Durang's caught us:] Here we are, at the end of a century of technologized urban life and mass-manufactured electronic entertainment, pretty much the same horrible creatures who laughed and cheered, a millennium and a half ago, while the Greek poets sang of the rapes of Zeus, the senseless butchery of the Trojan War, the frenzies of Cassandra, and the cruelty of Medea. We were there, in some form. We celebrated that. If you've read Aristophanes, you know that we laughed at it, too, and made brutal fun of Euripides and Socrates when they tried to look behind the laughter, and claimed that there was another side to the moral questions involved.

Many of Aristophanes's comedies are interrupted, just after their midpoint, by a convention called *parabasis*—literally, "walk down"—in which the chorus moves downstage center and talks directly to the audience, linking the play to the life around it, touching on current issues, naming names, and praising the author at the expense of his rivals. This isn't exactly what Christopher Durang does at the hilarious, astonishing moment when the chorus of *Betty's Summer Vacation* unexpectedly becomes visible; in fact, it's rather the opposite. Instead of telling the audience what to think, Durang's chorus is a sort of vocalized audience, telling his characters what we think—and sometimes coming alarmingly close to what we do think, at the very moment that we're thinking it.

Like the ancient Greek audience watching a myth unfold on the stage, these onstage spectators take the horrors and cruelties inside the play calmly, event-bites to be weighed for entertainment value, not for moral meaning. Yet they have a stringent, if capricious, moral system of their own, and its divergences from ours are the play's scariest aspect. (In Nicholas Martin's production, their costumes were capped with bits of the ceiling heating duct from which they emerged, making them look like segments of a large cartoon snake: the worm in the tequila bottle, maybe, or the serpent in the Garden.) The chorus graphs a specific series of public reactions to violent events, one which we know to be valid from real events — including some Durang mentions in the text— that have provoked similar public reactions. If they aren't identical to yours, you might well worry about what America has become; if they are, you might, seeing them, begin to worry about yourself. If your response includes elements of both, you might have a lot to worry about.

The chorus's reactions aren't the play's only measuring device. One of the characters—the chorus's favorite and usually the live audience's too—is named Mrs. Siezmagraff, a childlike distortion of the word *seismograph,* the electronic instrument that registers earthquake tremors. But Mrs. Siezmagraff doesn't register any outside tremors; she's an earthquake herself, constantly rattling the walls with her emotional vacillations and nonstop chatter. The measuring tool has become the destructive force it's supposed to measure. Traditionally our parents judge us, and we strive to live up to their standards; in Mrs. Siezmagraff's case, the parent has become more childlike than her own child, the judge has to be judged like anyone else.

Understandably in those circumstances, Mrs. Siezmagraff triumphs by becoming, in her maddest moment, judge, defendant, prosecutor, and unfriendly witness all at once. "The tragedy of our time," wrote Camus, "is that any of us can become, interchangeably, at any moment, victim or executioner." What's tragic, in due course, is also funny. Sometime in the late twentieth century, the endless tragedy that is human life, its sordid details endlessly recorded and reported by the all-observant media, became an endless comedy, as long as it was someone else's tragedy. Or sometimes even not: Think of the L.A. riots after the acquittal of the cops who assaulted Rodney King. Area residents watched buildings a few streets away burning down on TV, and then went outdoors to smell the smoke—or didn't.

The cops in *Betty's Summer Vacation* don't even bother to show up; the characters have to go to them to report even capital crimes. But they have no problem getting there and back. Unlike the real-world kind, the play's violence and madness are confined to the house. Which seems natural enough, given its owner's propensity toward madness. Yet we know that the streets out there are equally crazed; even if we didn't, the chorus would keep telling us. Earlier Durang plays, some of them autobiographical (like the harrowingly funny

The Marriage of Bette and Boo), have mapped the trauma of life with a mentally disturbed maternal figure; *Betty's Summer Vacation* is the first to declare the private madness in the house continuous with the madness outside. It's a playwright's way of declaring himself one with the world: In a demented society, all dementias are equally at home, though Mom gets priority rights on bravura display.

And the world, quadruply crazed now by its own self-awareness, was always a terrifying place. Not being born at all, as Sophocles said two and a half millennia before Beckett, would be the best thing. The Romanian-French philosopher E. M. Cioran put it even more strikingly: "What we find hardest is to forgive ourselves the terrible mistake of having been born." But we have to, in order to function as actors in life, rather than merely as audience. We have to walk away from the media circus, and clear our minds, and breathe. This has its own dangers: Somebody has to pay for the damage left behind by such circuses, and somebody has to clean up the inevitable mess.

Then, too, what we're breathing may be fraught with its own dangers. "I'm starting to feel better," Betty says, in the play's last line, and it's a proof of Durang's dignity as an artist that he doesn't cheapen the moment, à la Hollywood, with a scare-laugh of some kind. But, thinking of what might wash up on that peaceful beach—medical waste on the East Coast, oil and chemical spills on the West—we have every right to feel scared. Not for Betty, whom we know to be a fictional construct, but for ourselves. We live in the world that we've just seen refracted through that demented summer cottage. We know its little dangers as well as its big, less likely ones. And we know the audience that gapes interferingly at it whenever disaster strikes, hypocrite viewers, our likenesses and siblings. It's a small but genuine mercy that, thanks to Durang, we can laugh at it all—once we get over our nightmares.

The Cast

Betty's Summer Vacation had its premiere production off-Broadway on February 19, 1999 at Playwrights Horizons in New York City. Tim Sanford, artistic director; Leslie Marcus, managing director; Lynn Landis, general manager. The production was directed by Nicholas Martin; set design by Thomas Lynch; costumes by Michael Krass; lighting by Kevin Adams; sound by Kurt B. Kellenberger; original music by Peter Golub; and casting by James Calleri. The production manager was Christopher Boll, and the production stage manager was Kelley Kirkpatrick. The cast was as follows:

Betty	Kellie Overbey
Trudy	Julie Lund
Keith	Nat DeWolf
Mrs. Siezmagraff	Kristine Nielsen
Buck	Troy Sostillio
Mr. Vanislaw	Guy Boyd
Voice #1	Jack Ferver
Voice #2	Geneva Carr
Voice #3	Godfrey L. Simmons, Jr.

In June 1999, *Betty's Summer Vacation* won OBIE awards for playwriting, directing, set design, and acting (Kristine Nielsen).

Characters

BETTY
a nice, pretty normal young woman, late twenties.
Sensible, does her best to be reasonable.

TRUDY
friendly, chatty, needy, rather desperate underneath. Bit
younger than Betty.

KEITH
sensitive, quiet, mysterious. Late twenties. Finds it hard
to be around people. Seems sweet, seems weird.

BUCK
handsome, sexy lout-hunk. Might look like a beach guy
out of *Baywatch*. Unabashedly sexist, on the make all the
time.

MRS. SIEZMAGRAFF
lively, vibrant woman, mid-forties; oblivious to anyone
else's discomfort. Auntie Mame-ish.

MR. VANISLAW
an insane derelict who exposes himself to women in
bathrooms; naked except for raincoat and sneakers. A
little scary, but also just insane. Happy in his way.

THE GROUP OF VOICES
two men, one woman. They laugh, they applaud. They
live in the ceiling.

ACT ONE

SCENE ONE

Sound of the ocean.

A summer cottage, breezy-looking, inexpensive but functional summer furniture. Pleasant, soft colors, inviting.

An upstage door leads in from the front of the cottage. Inside there are a number of doors, leading off to bedrooms—four doors in a cluster, one by itself. (Some of the doors can be implied in an offstage hallway, if need be). There is a door off-left that leads to an outdoor deck and the outside.

Primarily a living room, but an open kitchen is also part of it.

A woman BETTY, age twenty-nine, comes in with her friend TRUDY, age twenty-eight. They are carrying suitcases.

Betty Wow. This house is great.

Trudy Isn't it? I knew you'd like it.

Betty (*going off to look*) Oh, and it has a great deck. And you can almost see the ocean.

Comes back inside.

Trudy I know. It's a comfy house. I love that. It's so great to be out of the city. The pace is so much slower here. Smell the air. There's salt in the air. It's from the ocean. I love the ocean. I am so sick of cement in the city. You smell the air in the city and you smell car exhaust and those fat unhealthy pretzels that those vendors sell in midtown. But here, it's all healthy. I can't wait to eat only healthy food. What is tofu exactly? Well, we don't have to eat tofu. We just have to eat vegetables and fish and maybe chicken, but not put butter on anything, well maybe on a piece of bread with some sugar on it, do you ever do that, my mother taught me to do it, isn't it gross, but it gives me energy, gee, I really love the seashore.

Betty (*polite, trying not to offend*) Trudy, I've told you I hoped you wouldn't talk too much on this vacation.

Trudy Really?

> *Trudy tries for a few seconds to be quiet. Betty looks around, checking out the various bedrooms. Trudy starts talking again pretty soon.*

What day is today, Saturday? What a long ride it was in the car, traffic really freaks me out, everyone in these cars, trapped, unable to move, did you ever see Fellini's *8½*, that's what happens in the beginning of the movie, but then Marcello Mastroianni, he's so handsome, why aren't there any American men like him, I'd marry them in a minute if they'd have me, but lots of men don't like it if you talk too much, but I could probably have my mouth wired shut, at least if it was Marcello Mastroianni . . . anyway, he's in this traffic jam, and nobody's moving at all, and eventually he just rises up and floats up out of the car and it looks like he's escaping the awful traffic jam, but then it turns out someone has attached a rope to his leg, and so he's really still tied to the earth, and it doesn't look like he's going to escape at all.

Betty Uh-huh. Listening to you is like listening to the radio.

Trudy Really, I wonder if I should have a show?

Betty Now I want you to practice quiet. Pretend you're a monk or nun or something and you have to follow the Grand Silence. Can you do that?

Trudy Sure! Which bedroom should I have? Which one is closest to the sound of the ocean? I love to listen to the ocean.

Betty How can you even hear it when you're talking?

Trudy Well, I hear it right underneath my talking, it's kind of like they say, if you have a puppy and you're training it to sleep alone on a blanket, you should put a ticking clock next to it and it'll think it's its mother breathing, but I don't think a puppy is that stupid, do you, and plus it certainly wouldn't work with a human, I'd either think this is a ticking bomb, or I'd think this clock is too loud, I won't be able to sleep with this racket, maybe I should order a pizza. Isn't it scary about germ warfare?

Betty What does a pizza have to do with anything?

Trudy Well, you know if I was hungry. I don't suppose there's food here, is there? We probably have to go to the store. I love to go to the supermarkets outside of the city, the aisles are so wide and comfortable, and the checkout people say "thank you" and so on.

Betty Yes, we'll have to go shopping. I think I need aspirin. And maybe ear stoppers.

Trudy Then you won't be able to hear the ocean. I love hearing the ocean. I'm so glad to be away form the sound of the city. Car alarms. Has a car alarm ever stopped a car from being stolen? I doubt it. It just goes on and on. (*she begins to imitate various car alarms*) Oooooo-oooo. Ooooooooo-ooooo. Waaahhhh-ahhhhh, waaaaaaaa-ahhhhh. Wuuuuuu-uuuulp! Wuuuuuu-uuuulp!

Betty Why don't you take a nap?

Trudy I just got here, I'm too full of energy. (*looks toward entrance door*) Oh, look, here comes another roommate, or maybe he's a serial killer, I hope not.

Enter KEITH. He carries a large shovel, and a hatbox, and a suitcase. He's twenty-eight to thirty-two years old, fairly attractive, dressed in khakis and a plain sports shirt.

Keith Hi, I'm Keith. Are you Helen and Susie?

Trudy No, I'm Trudy, and this is Betty.

Betty Hi.

Trudy I hope you're not a serial killer, and that shovel's for burying people. And what's in the hatbox? Not a head, I hope. That's another old movie I like, *Night Must Fall,* with Robert Montgomery, he's Elizabeth Montgomery's father from *Bewitched,* isn't it amazing how many children of people in show business go on to have successful careers, like talent is genetic for real, as well as, of course, it opens doors for you if your parent is in show business . . . well, he keeps a head in a hat for the whole movie, and then you find out that's what he's been doing. Gosh, you look startled. Is it because I've said something outlandish, or is it because you really are a serial killer and you're guilty?

Keith (*looking startled*) No. I'm not looking startled. Please don't look in the hatbox, it's private. It has . . . hats in it. And I go everywhere with a shovel because what if my car gets caught in a snowdrift.

Trudy But it's summer.

Keith Well . . . eventually it will be winter again. And plus, my car could get caught in a sand dune.

Trudy Uh-huh.

Betty Why did you ask if we were Helen and Susie?

Keith I'm sorry. I meant Betty and Trudy, I guess. I mean, I've never met you, I've only met the owner of the cottage, Mrs. Siezmagraff.

4

Betty Oh.

Trudy Wow. You're really cute. Do you have a girlfriend?

Keith I believe in celibacy.

Trudy stares at him. Silence.

Betty Well, that shut her up.

Keith I'd like to go to my room now. Do you know where it is?

Betty We haven't chosen rooms yet. Why don't we go look and see what we want. (*points*) There are these four together, and then that one over there by itself.

Keith kind of bolts over to the room by itself, and goes into it, shutting the door behind him. Trudy sits down, stunned. She starts to cry.

Betty What's the matter?

Trudy I think he's horrible. What does he mean, he believes in celibacy. Is he a monk or something? And what's in the hatbox? And why does he have a shovel? Maybe he really is a serial killer.

Sound of LAUGHTER, like on a television sitcom. Trudy and Betty hear it, and look disoriented.

Did you just hear something?

Betty It sounded like a laugh track.

Trudy Oh, God, he's weird . . . he's brought a taped recording of people laughing. What's the matter with him?

Sound of LAUGHTER.

Betty I don't think it's him. (*knocks on door*) Keith, you're not playing a tape of anything, are you?

Keith (*off*) I'm busy now, I can't talk.

Trudy Why is he so weird?

LAUGHTER.

Enter MRS. SIEZMAGRAFF. She is forty-five to fifty-five, a vibrant woman in bright clothes. She has a large sun hat on, and sunglasses.

Mrs. Siezmagraff Hi, everyone. Isn't the cottage great? Have you chosen your bedrooms yet? I want the smallest one, I shouldn't really even be here, but my husband just died and we lost the house, and I don't really have anywhere else to live but here. Plus I love young people anyway.

LAUGHTER.

Betty (*focused more on Mrs. Siezmagraff than on the laughter right now*) What?

Mrs. Siezmagraff What was that laughter? Did you hear it?

Trudy I think it's laughter from a sitcom.

Mrs. Siezmagraff Oh. Well, that's all right then. So, are you surprised to see me?

Betty Well, yes, I mean, aren't you renting the house *to* us? Do you mean, you're going to be staying here with us?

Mrs. Siezmagraff Yes, isn't it a kick?

Trudy We're afraid Keith may be a serial killer.

Mrs. Siezmagraff Oh, well, I'll know when I meet him. I'm a very good judge of character, especially men's characters. My husband died of cirrhosis of the liver. Do you think he was an alcoholic? All my friends do. I could never tell. Sometimes he'd beat me, but you know, he was always sorry, so I always forgave him. Forgiving is important, don't you think?

Betty I'm sorry. I find that you and Trudy seem to talk similarly. Why is that?

Mrs. Siezmagraff Well, she's my daughter.

Trudy Oh, Mom, I didn't want anyone to know!

Trudy slams off to her room. LAUGHTER.

Betty You're Trudy's mother?

Mrs. Siezmagraff Yes. But we don't talk much because her father incested her when he was drunk, and I never did anything about it because I was codependent. I mean, what should I have done? Broken up the family and gone on welfare?

Betty Uh-huh. You're Trudy's mother?

Mrs. Siezmagraff No, not really. Well, yes, but we haven't worked it through yet. She doesn't like to see me.

Betty Well, when you said your husband died, why didn't Trudy react?

Mrs. Siezmagraff She's very disconnected from her feelings. That's why she talks so much. Even in the cradle. Gee gee gee, ga ga ga. On and on she went, saying absolutely nothing. It was real annoying. We used to leave her alone for hours at a time, and just put this big clicking clock next to her. Wow, I'm starved, is there any food yet?

Betty No, we haven't gone to the store yet.

Mrs. Siezmagraff Well, when you go, get me about twelve bagels, I eat them all the time, there's no fat in them, you know.

Betty Bagels, right. You know, I just thought about something. Haven't you already met Keith? I mean the one you said you'd know if he was a serial killer when you met him. Didn't you meet him when he applied for a share in the house? I thought you met all of us.

Mrs. Siezmagraff Yeah, I met him. Which one was he? The big macho one or the sort of sensitive one with the hatbox.

Betty He's the one with a hatbox.

Mrs. Siezmagraff Oh, I don't think he's a serial killer. Do you? Does he say he is? It isn't Trudy who thinks he's a killer, is it? She thought her father was a sex pervert, and he wasn't. He was just drunk. So she exaggerates. I don't believe anything Trudy says, she's worthless. (*calls out toward Trudy's door*) No, she's wonderful!

Makes face at Betty—"well, I tried."

But I think Keith is fine. Don't you? Is he here?

Knocks on Keith's door.

Hi Keith. How are you? It's Mrs. Siezmagraff, I'm here to share the summer with you all, isn't that great? Keith? (*back to Betty*) Well, he's quiet. Gosh, since I'm here, there'll be one less bedroom. Well, maybe one of the people due to be here will be killed in a car crash. Although traffic was moving very slowly. Maybe there'll be an earthquake. Except we're on the East Coast, not the West Coast. Of course, there are earthquakes on the East Coast.

Betty Please, I feel you're talking too much.

Mrs. Siezmagraff Well, fuck you!

Mrs. Siezmagraff storms to Keith's room, slams the door. Inside she and Keith both scream. She comes out of the room. Goes to another door, goes inside, slams it shut.

Enter BUCK. He's the "macho" one . . . handsome, muscular, in jeans and sleeveless T-shirt. He carries weights and a six-pack of beer.

Buck Hi, there, I'm Buck. Where's the party?

Betty Well, this is it, I guess. Hi, I'm Betty.

Buck Hi. I'm Buck. Wanna beer?

Betty No, thank you. It's sort of early in the morning.

Buck Yeah? Think I'll have a brew. Hold this, would you?

He hands her a weight; she holds it, it drops down to the ground due to its heaviness. LAUGHTER. He opens a beer, which was why he handed her the weight. He hears the laughter.

What was that?

Betty I don't know. There seems to be a laugh track in the house.

Buck Cool. Do you like flavored condoms?

Betty No, I don't. I prefer that people get tested first.

Buck picks the weights back up, sips his beer.

Buck Yeah, but then they could go have sex right after the test, so you never know really, do you? When you go to the store, get me some condoms, okay? I only got twenty-five left. Where should I put my weights?

Betty I don't know. On the ground?

LAUGHTER. Buck comes up very close to Betty; his body is inappropriately close to hers. Very seductive.

Buck I mean, which room is mine.

Betty (*flustered*) Oh. Well, there are two left . . . that one and that one.

Buck If you don't point when you say "that one and that one," I don't know which ones you mean.

Betty Oh, sorry. There's this one here, and the one at the end of the hall on the left.

LAUGHTER.

Buck Great. You wanna have sex?

Betty Really, I just met you.

Buck Well, if you change your mind, I haven't got my rocks off since this morning.

Betty It is this morning.

Buck Well, since earlier this morning.

LAUGHTER.

That laughter is kind of annoying. Can you do anything to control it?

Betty I don't think so.

Buck (*looks up; shouts*) Shut up! (*to Betty*) Well, see you later.

He exits to his room.

Betty is momentarily overwhelmed by the people she's just met. Almost has to shake off the strange energy. Maybe we hear the sound of the ocean again.

Betty (*to herself*) Gosh, there's only one room left ... and there's still another person to come ... Abigail, I think.

Phone rings.

Hello? Who? Who died? Oh, a car accident.

LAUGHTER. Betty looks shocked that the laugh track laughed at this. Refocuses on call.

Gee, that's a shame. Is this Abigail's mother? No? Her masseuse? Really. Were you in the car with her? Uh-huh. Well, were you massaging her while she was driving? Really? No, I'm not saying you caused the accident. I'm just saying I think a massage should be given on a massage table and not in a moving vehicle. Well, perhaps I am rigid. But I'm not dead either, am I? Hello ... hello. (*feeling oddly bad, even though no one is there anymore*) Sorry. (*hangs up*) Gosh, how strange.

LAUGHTER.

Betty looks up toward the laughter.

End Scene

SCENE TWO

> *Later that day. Trudy and Buck come in from outside, in wet bathing suits, drying themselves.*

Trudy Oh, the ocean was so refreshing.

Buck Yeah, it was great.

Trudy Oh, I love being out of the city. It's so fresh here by the ocean. You know, where life began, with the fish crawling out of the water and developing backbones and then becoming monkeys or dinosaurs and then eventually humans.

Buck What? Yeah. You're real pretty, you know that.

Trudy Thank you. (*to herself*) My father always thought so.

Buck Well, he was right.

Trudy He just died, apparently.

Buck Really? That's cool. I mean, that's too bad. What do you mean, "apparently"?

Trudy Well, Mrs. Siezmagraff told me.

Buck Uh-huh. Wow, all this talk about the ocean is making me horny.

Trudy We weren't talking about the ocean, we were talking about death.

Buck Whatever.

> *LAUGHTER.*

Shut up!

Trudy Were you ever molested by you parents?

Buck Is this kind of foreplay talk? Wow, you're kinky.

Trudy No, it's not kinky, I'm opening up my soul to you.

Buck Don't do that. Open up your bathing suit to me.

Trudy It doesn't open up, it comes off. You're a pig.

Buck Oink, oink. You wanna brew?

Trudy Brew? You mean, beer?

Buck Whatever.

Trudy Cool, whatever, brew. I hate the way you talk. You're an idiot.

Buck I don't care. Let's just have sex, okay?

Trudy You're just like my father.

Buck Wow. Kinky.

Trudy It's not kinky, it's pathetic.

Buck Whatever turns you on.

Trudy Stop saying that. Nothing turns me on. I like Keith more than I like you. He's more sensitive.

Knocks on Keith's door.

Keith, do you want to come out and talk for a while? Buck is bothering me.

Keith (*off*) I'm busy now.

Trudy Well, can't you come out?

Keith comes out with rubber gloves on, which seem to be bloody.

Keith I'm doing an operation now. What do you want?

Trudy (*taken aback; tries to act normal*) Oh, I'm sorry. I just wanted some company.

Keith Well, I'm sorry. Now isn't a good time.

LAUGHTER. Keith goes back in his room.

Buck Keith is pretty weird, huh?

Trudy Yeah. What did he mean, an operation?

Buck I don't know. You know, what a doctor does. He must be a doctor. Or veterinarian.

Trudy Yeah. He could be a veterinarian.

Knocks on Keith's door.

Keith, are you a veterinarian?

Keith (*off*) I can't talk now. Leave me alone.

Buck Wow. I've got a boner. Wanna see?

Trudy Please, you're disgusting.

Buck Oh, you love it. Here, feel it.

Trudy Stop it. This is sexual harassment.

Buck Yeah, I love that stuff. Did you see *Oleanna*? It was this cool play about sexual harassment. I loved it when the guy finally punched that bitch. POW, POW! Right in the chops. That was a good play.

Trudy I didn't see it.

Buck I have pictures of my penis. Do you want to see them?

Trudy No, I don't. You have pictures??? Yes, I would like to see them.

Buck They're in my room. Hold on a sec.

Buck bounds out to his bedroom.

Trudy I'm glad you're dead, Daddy! I'm glad!

LAUGHTER.

What's funny about that?

Laugh Track Voices (*speaking as a group*) It sounded corny.

Trudy screams at the sound of the group speaking. LAUGHTER. Enter Buck carrying a very large photo album.

Buck Here are my dick pix.

They sit on the couch, look at his photo album.

Buck This is when it's only semierect. And this is a morning hard-on. And this is me pissing.

Trudy Mmmm, very nice . . . I think I don't want to see any more pictures of your penis.

Buck Makin' ya hungry for the real thing, huh?

Trudy No . . . that's really very far from what I was thinking. I think I want to become a lesbian.

Buck Cool. I could dig it with two chicks.

Trudy I want to talk about religion. Unitarianism seems a nice religion. Put your penis away, please.

She closes the photo album.

Buck Oh, you're a tease. I'm so horny now, ya gotta help me, Trudy.

Buck starts to nuzzle her. Trudy pulls away. Betty comes in, carrying several bags of groceries.

Betty I'm back.

Buck Hi. You get the beer and the condoms?

Betty Yes, Buck, I did.

Buck Cool. I got a ragin' hard-on.

Betty Really. Maybe you could get shots of estrogen, and it might subside.

Buck Yeah. You wish.

Trudy Betty, have you seen Mrs. Siezmagraff?

Betty You mean, your mother? No, isn't she here?

Trudy I don't know where she is. (*to Buck*) Should we tell her about Keith?

Buck Keith? What about him?

Trudy Well, how he seemed when he came out of his room.

Buck How did he seem?

Trudy Well, he had on bloody rubber gloves. Why were they bloody?

Betty What?

Trudy Keith had on bloody rubber gloves.

Betty Goodness. Why?

Buck Well, to protect his hands, probably.

    LAUGHTER.

Shut up!

Betty Oh dear. I have a queasy feeling about Keith.

Buck You're probably just horny. You wanna get it on? Trudy's bein' a fuckin' cock tease.

Betty You're totally gross.

LAUGHTER

In what way is that funny?

Laugh Track Voices (*speaking as a group*) It was so true it was funny.

Betty and Trudy both scream. Buck is also bothered to hear them speak.

Buck Shut up!

Enter Mrs. Siezmagraff in beach caftan.

Mrs. Siezmagraff Hi, everybody. I just got stung by a stingray.

Mrs. Siezmagraff collapses on the floor in a heap.

LAUGHTER.

Everyone stares down at her. Keith comes out of his door, still with his bloody gloves on. He joins the others in looking down at the collapsed Mrs. Siezmagraff.

More LAUGHTER.

End Scene

SCENE THREE

Evening. Preparations for a nice dinner. Candlelight. Betty is cooking. The dinner setup is probably best set offstage, on the deck area.

Mrs. Siezmagraff comes out, all dressed up in a floor-length gown that hides her legs. She looks pretty, if probably a bit garish.

Mrs. Siezmagraff (*to Betty*) I have these enormous red welts on my upper thighs. It's really unfortunate. I guess if I have sexual relations with Mr. Vanislaw, we better keep the lights off. Or he could be blindfolded, I guess. I've never done that, but people find it exciting, I'm told.

Checking what Betty is cooking; or nibbling on something.

I once saw this movie about a sorority hazing, and they showed these freshman girls this bowl of wiggling worms, then they blindfolded them and fed them what they assumed was the worms, but it was really just spaghetti, but the girls didn't know that and they choked and vomited and just had a terrible time.

Betty A sorority hazing. How unusual.

Mrs. Siezmagraff Yeah, I guess so. I have no idea what the movie was. I think that was the only scene of it I saw. It seemed to be from the fifties. I think the difference between the innocence of then versus now is that now they'd just go ahead and feed them the worms and not bother about switching to spaghetti. Isn't that sad? I feel something's been lost. But, oh well, we have someone coming to dinner, so I shouldn't let my feelings plummet down to the cellar, should I? La dee dah, oh for the life of a swan. Is that the saying? Oh, for the life of a something.

Betty Who is this Mr. Vanislaw?

Mrs. Siezmagraff Well, I found him hiding in the women's changing room. He had a camera and was taking pictures.

Betty looks alarmed; Mrs. Siezmagraff is happily oblivious.

He said it was harmless, just for his personal use. Some of the women hit him, but I think, you know, "different strokes for different folks." That's such a good phrase, don't you think? I like men who like women; they're my favorite kind. Oh, that Buck here is real cute, don't you think?

Betty I think he's an idiot.

Mrs. Siezmagraff Really? Well, everyone tells me I have bad taste in men.

Looks out to deck; happy

Oh, here comes Mr. Vanislaw now. Yoo-hoo, over here!

MR. VANISLAW enters. He is over forty. He is wearing a raincoat and nothing else except sneakers. He is maybe unshaven. Very unsavory.

Mr. Vanislaw Hi, there, baby, what's hanging?

With his back to the audience, he opens up his raincoat and exposes himself to Mrs. Siezmagraff. She seems enchanted. Betty screams in horror.

LAUGHTER.

Mrs. Siezmagraff Oh, Mr. Vanislaw, you're a card.

Looks closer, near his genital area.

What an interesting tattoo. Is that the devil? I love where his pitchfork is pointing, it's very playful.

Betty Mrs. Siezmagraff, you've brought a derelict into the house. And a sex maniac.

Mr. Vanislaw Look at my dicky!

He shakes himself at Betty; we still only see his back.

Betty Really, I can't permit this. Please close your raincoat.

Mrs. Siezmagraff Oh, Mr. Vanislaw ... not everyone has a sense of humor, so maybe you better keep your raincoat closed, at least for now. Oh, I want you to meet my daughter. She's taking a nap in her room. Why don't you go in there and introduce yourself to her?

Mr. Vanislaw All right.

With energy and purpose, Mr. Vanislaw goes into Trudy's room.

Betty Mrs. Siezmagraff, I must protest. Have you no sense of what's appropriate?

Terrible screams from Trudy's room. Trudy comes rushing out, hysterical. Mr. Vanislaw follows behind, redoing his raincoat, laughing.

Mr. Vanislaw She didn't like my devil tattoo.

Trudy Someone broke into my room!

Mrs. Siezmagraff Trudy, don't exaggerate. No one broke into your room, it wasn't even locked. And this is Mr. Vanislaw, he's our dinner guest.

Trudy Are you insane?

Mrs. Siezmagraff Why do people ask me that all the time? It's so rude. No, I'm not insane. Do I seem insane to you? And if I was insane, would I necessarily know it? I doubt it. So it's a really meaningless question. Mr. Vanislaw, do you think I'm insane?

Mr. Vanislaw Where's the person with the head in the box?

Mrs. Siezmagraff Well, now, we don't know that there's a head in the box. It could just be hats.

Mr. Vanislaw Where is he, where is he?

LAUGHTER.

Mr. Vanislaw briefly notices the laugher, but then focuses on trying to find the room of the person he's been told about. However, he manages to go into all the wrong rooms.

Mrs. Siezmagraff Now don't you go molesting him. Unlike my daughter, he's a boy, and it's not nice for a gentleman to molest a boy.

Trudy I don't understand. And it is all right for a man to molest a girl.

Mrs. Siezmagraff Well, it's certainly more normal, I'm sure you'll grant me that.

Mr. Vanislaw (*at Betty's room*) Is this his room?

Mrs. Siezmagraff No, no, it's over there.

Mrs. Siezmagraff points to Keith's room.

Mr. Vanislaw (*opening the door, happy, playful*) Helloooooooooooo there, I've come to get you.

Mr. Vanislaw lets himself into Keith's room. Long silence. Everyone listens.

Mrs. Siezmagraff Well, they seem to be getting along fine.

Trudy Mother, why did you bring this person back to dinner?

Mrs. Siezmagraff Well, for company for me. Your father's dead. I need some male companionship.

Knocks on Keith's door.

Don't you be too long in there, Mr. Vanislaw. You're my guest, don't forget. I'm not quite sure why everyone finds Keith so fascinating.

Trudy Well, he's sensitive and withdrawn. Sensible women like that.

Betty I wonder if we should call the police about Keith.

Mrs. Siezmagraff I don't think so. He might interpret that wrong.

Knocks on Keith's door.

I hope you're not dismembering bodies or anything in there.

LAUGHTER.

Betty (*annoyed at the laughter*) In what way is that funny?

Voices We're uncomfortable. And so we laughed. We didn't know what else to do.

Betty Oh. Odd.

Mrs. Siezmagraff Did anyone else just hear voices from the ceiling?

Betty It's the people who've been laughing. They seem to be talking from time to time now.

Mrs. Siezmagraff Oh. Well, if I'm the only one hearing it, maybe it's a reaction to being stung by the stingray.

Betty But you're not the only one hearing it.

Mrs. Siezmagraff Well, no one else seemed to hear it.

Trudy Mother, we all heard it.

Mrs. Siezmagraff Well, you're not a very reliable witness, Trudy. After all, you said your father forced you to have sex with him.

Trudy He did.

Mrs. Siezmagraff Well, that's not what he told me. He said you seduced him.

Trudy Mother, I was underage.

Mrs. Siezmagraff It's never too young to be a flirt. Flirting with your father . . . it's disgusting. Why do you insist on being so competitive with me?

Trudy My therapist says I shouldn't even talk to you. And that it's impossible to debate anything with you because you're insane and you're sick.

Mrs. Siezmagraff Betty, do you talk to your mother this way?

Betty No. But I wasn't molested by my father.

Mrs. Siezmagraff Well, neither was Trudy.

Trudy I was too.

Mrs. Siezmagraff Was not!

Trudy Was too!

Mrs. Siezmagraff Was not!

LAUGHTER.

MRS. SIEZMAGRAFF (*to LAUGHTER; irritated*) Why is that funny?

Voices You were arguing about something very serious in a childish way, and it made us laugh.

Mrs. Siezmagraff Well, you're just a bunch of insensitive boobs, that's all I can say.

Enter Buck.

Buck Someone say something about boobs?

Mrs. Siezmagraff Oh hello, Buck. Aren't you attractive this evening? Tell me, you find me more attractive than my daughter, Trudy, don't you?

Trudy Mother!

Trudy storms off to her room.

Mrs. Siezmagraff Trudy always overreacts to everything. (*to Buck*) And she's not good at putting out. While I am. We can keep the lights off so you don't see the welts from the sting-ray.

Buck Cool.

Betty Mrs. Siezmagraff, I'm shocked!

Mrs. Siezmagraff Well, my husband's dead, my daughter is rude to me, and God knows when Mr. Vanislaw is coming out of that room with Keith. So what else do you expect me to do?

Betty I expect you to eat dinner and make pleasant conversation.

Mrs. Siezmagraff We'll microwave the dinner up later. Come on, Buck. Let me show you some tricks I learned when I visited my husband in prison.

Buck Cool.

Buck and Mrs. Siezmagraff go off to Mrs. Siezmagraff's room. Betty looks around the room.

Betty But I've worked so hard on dinner. (*starts to cry*)

Voices (*in sympathy*) Awwwww............

Betty looks startled at their sound. Not sure she likes getting sympathy from them. Looks confused.

End Scene

SCENE FOUR

After dinner. Everyone is playing charades: Mrs. Siezmagraff, Buck, Trudy, Betty.

Keith is also present, but uncomfortable to be in a large group and unhappy to be part of a game. He has his arms wrapped around himself. He mostly just watches what happens, but otherwise tries not to interact much.

Betty is in the midst of her turn, which has been going on for a while. She is presently acting out a sneeze, but pulls on her ear to signal that it's a "sounds like" clue.

Trudy Sneeze!!?

Mrs. Siezmagraff No, sounds like sneeze. Knees?

Buck Keys?

Mrs. Siezmagraff Fleas. March something fleas.

Betty shakes her head no.

Trudy Not fleas.

Buck Sleaze!

Betty shakes her head no.

Not sleaze.

Mrs. Siezmagraff Rhymes with sneeze. Everything rhymes with sneeze. I'm sick of this word. Go back to the fifth word again.

Betty holds up five fingers for the fifth word. Then taps her forearm with one finger, meaning first syllable.

Trudy Sssssh, fifth word again. First syllable.

Betty acts "cold"—shivering, etc.

Mrs. Siezmagraff Cold. Freezing.

Buck Fucking cold.

Trudy Shiver. Shiver me timbers.

Mrs. Siezmagraff March of the Something Shiver. Shiva.

Betty shakes her head. Changes her "cold" routine to acting like she's getting sudden chills, so she will be still, then will shudder suddenly.

Mrs. Siezmagraff Shock treatments.

Betty shakes her head. Does a sudden cold chill again.

Trudy Sudden chills!

Betty nods enthusiastically, points to Trudy.

Sudden chills. Chills. March of the Something Chills.

Buck *March of the Big Chills.* That movie was cool.

Trudy March of the Chill. March of the Children. "March of the Siamese Children"!

Betty Yes! Finally!

Trudy Hooray!

Buck What's "March of the Siamese Children"?

Trudy Didn't you ever see *The King and I*?

Buck What? Shakespeare?

Mrs. Siezmagraff Maybe we should have a time limit. That took half an hour to get.

Betty I thought it would never end.

Trudy You did very well.

Mrs. Siezmagraff Whose turn is it—Keith's?

Keith looks horrified, makes whimpering sounds.

Well, your turn is soon, Keith. But maybe Mr. Vanislaw can go next. Where is Mr. Vanislaw?

Trudy Mother, he's in the bathroom in Buck's room. Let's just leave him there.

Mrs. Siezmagraff Well, what's he doing there for half an hour?

Crosses toward Buck's room; calling out.

Mr. Vanislaw, we miss you. It's your turn. Are you going to come out soon?

Exits into Buck's room.

Trudy I think something's wrong with Mr. Vanislaw.

Buck I think he's funny. He's a coot.

Trudy Well, Keith doesn't seem to like him. Keith, you didn't like Mr. Vanislaw, did you?

Keith looks up at her and shakes his head.

What did the two of you do in there for so long?

Keith shrugs.

LAUGHTER.

What was funny, I don't understand.

Group of Voices We were thinking of something else.

Keith looks startled. He's never heard the voices speak before. The others are blasé about it by now.

Trudy Well, please pay attention to us if you're going to laugh, please.

Buck God, this is a weird house.

Enter Mrs. Siezmagraff, dragging Mr. Vanislaw by the hand.

Mrs. Siezmagraff Someone's going to have to mop up in there after Mr. Vanislaw. I don't know what the hell he was doing.

LAUGHTER.

Trudy Mother, why can't you have normal friends?

Mrs. Siezmagraff Well, why can't I have a normal daughter? Okay, where's a piece of paper for Mr. Vanislaw?

Betty offers Mrs. Siezmagraff the bowl of papers with charades titles on them. Mrs. Siezmagraff reaches in and hands Mr. Vanislaw a piece of paper.

Now can you read, or are you on drugs?

Mr. Vanislaw I can read. It says . . .

Mrs. Siezmagraff No, don't tell us. Make us say the word by silent clues. This is charades. Remember, we explained it to you before you went to the bathroom. Remember, Buck acted out "Nutcracker Suite."

Mr. Vanislaw (*likes the word*) Nuts.

Starts to undo his coat.

Mrs. Siezmagraff That's right, nuts. Now keep your raincoat closed, Mr. Vanislaw, Betty and Trudy have made a special request.

Mr. Vanislaw They're very controlling.

Mrs. Siezmagraff Yes, they are. Keith, are you paying attention? Mr. Vanislaw is about to give clues.

Keith hunches up and looks frightened, looks away.

Well, listen closely then, Keith. If you have any ideas, just call them out. Okay, we'll start now. Mr. Vanislaw, begin now.

Mr. Vanislaw laughs energetically, then holds up one finger, hoping someone will say "one."

Mrs. Siezmagraff Wait, wait, tell us what we're going for. Is this a song title, or a title of a book, or a movie title, or what?

Mr. Vanislaw looks at the paper, then shrugs, not knowing.

Well, fine, so we're going for something, but we don't know what. Okay, that's fine.

Trudy Why does he have to have a turn? He's a derelict.

Mrs. Siezmagraff Darling, don't you use that word, it's rude to Mr. Vanislaw. Go ahead, Mr. Vanislaw.

Mr. Vanislaw holds up index finger, for the word "one."

Mrs. Siezmagraff First word.

Mr. Vanislaw continues to hold up index finger.

Yes, we got it. This is the first word. Now give us a clue.

Mr. Vanislaw This is a clue. What I'm doing.

Mrs. Siezmagraff Oh.

Buck Finger.

Mr. Vanislaw No, not finger.

Mrs. Siezmagraff Don't speak, just shake your head.

Mr. Vanislaw shakes his head "no."

First word. Not finger. Index finger. Index. Index of Forbidden Books.

Mr. Vanislaw shakes his head "no."

Betty One. Is it the number one?

Mr. Vanislaw Yes!

Mrs. Siezmagraff Mr. Vanislaw, no talking. Just nod yes or no, please.

Mr. Vanislaw nods "yes" energetically. Then he starts taking his finger and "touching" his arm, to communicate the word "touch."

What is this, the second word? Say second word.

Mr. Vanislaw Second word.

Mrs. Siezmagraff No, don't say it. Hold up two fingers for second word.

Annoyed, Mr. Vanislaw holds up two fingers.

Second word. All right. Now give us the clue.

Mr. Vanislaw again gives the "touching" clue.

Buck Arm.

Betty Wrist.

Mr. Vanislaw shakes his head "no."

Mrs. Siezmagraff Skin? Well, what are you doing? You keep touching your arm. Is it arm?

Mr. Vanislaw nods energetically and points at Mrs. Siezmagraff because she said "touch."

It is arm?

Annoyed, Mr. Vanislaw shakes his head "no."

Well, you nodded "yes."

Betty (*trying hard in order to get the game to end*) Touching your arm.

Mr. Vanislaw points to her, nods "yes."

Touching. Touch?

Mrs. Siezmagraff One touch.

Buck One-touch banking?

Mr. Vanislaw shakes his head. Pulls his ear for a "sounds like."

Mrs. Siezmagraff Sounds like. Very good. Is this the third word?

Mr. Vanislaw nods his head. Does "sounds like" gesture again. Then, with his back to audience, he opens his raincoat and points to his genitals.

Betty and Trudy are horrified. Keith just stares. Buck laughs. Mrs. Siezmagraff is annoyed.

LAUGHTER. Applause.

Mr. Vanislaw, we told you, no more flashing at people. We're playing a game now. There's a time for everything, and this isn't the time now.

Trudy Get him out of here!

Mrs. Siezmagraff Oh, Trudy, you're such a withered prune.

Mr. Vanislaw keeps pointing to his genitals, going up to people and pointing.

Yes. We see it. Thank you. Now put it away. We're playing a game.

Mr. Vanislaw I know we're playing a game! This is a clue. Sounds like what I'm pointing at.

Mrs. Siezmagraff Oh. Well, that's all right, then, I guess. Girls, it's a clue, he's not being inappropriate now, after all.

Buck One Touch Dick.

Mrs. Siezmagraff No, sounds like, so it couldn't be dick. One Touch Mick. Pick. Lick. Sick.

Betty *One Touch of Venus.*

Mrs. Siezmagraff What?

Betty The clue is penis. *One Touch of Venus.*

Mr. Vanislaw Yes!!

Mr. Vanislaw is delighted, and starts to dance around happily, still with his back to the audience and with his coat undone.

Buck What's *One Touch of Venus?* A porno flick?

Betty Well, in Mr. Vanislaw's version, I'm sure it is. Please close your coat now, Mr. Vanislaw, we guessed your title.

Mr. Vanislaw's victory dance is becoming less a dance and more just his shaking his member upstage.

Keith has a very clear view of Mr. Vanislaw's gyrations. Keith is initially embarrassed, and looks away. But then he keeps looking back up, and soon he starts to smile a bit and enjoy Mr. Vanislaw's shaking of his genitals.

The other characters are presently not paying much attention to Mr. Vanislaw.

Mrs. Siezmagraff (*to Betty*) Well. He did very well, then, didn't he? He got that much faster than you got "March of the Siamese Children," I must say.

Buck (Troy Sostillio) arrives at his summer share with beer and weights. There seems to be laughter coming from the ceiling.

All photographs of the 1999 off Broadway production of
Betty's Summer Vacation by Joan Marcus.

Mr. Vanislaw, naked underneath his raincoat, tries to play
charades. Left to right: Guy Boyd, Kellie Overbey,
Troy Sostillio, Nat DeWolf, Julie Lund, and Kristine Nielsen
as Mrs. Siezmagraff.

Mrs. Siezmagraff (Kristine Nielsen) is perplexed when 911
calls her back.

The Voices demand to be entertained.
Left to right: Nat DeWolf, Kristine Nielsen,
Jack Ferver, Geneva Carr and Godfrey Simmons, Jr.

Betty This is the stupidest game of charades I've ever played. Let's call it quits. I want to do the dishes.

Mrs. Siezmagraff No, no, you made the dinner, I think Trudy should do the dishes.

Trudy Mother!

Mrs. Siezmagraff suddenly sees Mr. Vanislaw still shaking himself.

Mrs. Siezmagraff Mr. Vanislaw!!!! Close your coat now.

Mr. Vanislaw finally closes his coat. Keith stops smiling and looks slightly "caught."

We've all gotten the penis clue, it's time to move on to other things now.

Everyone calms down. Mrs. Siezmagraff and Mr. Vanislaw sit down for a moment.

Keith, you're awfully silent, do you have nothing to say?

Keith I was abused as a child. The memories are starting to come back to me. I think that's why I cut people's heads off.

No one moves. He gets up and goes to his room. Silence. Everyone is blank-faced.

Mrs. Siezmagraff Well, who's going to do the dishes?

Buck I'll do 'em. Maybe you and Mr. Vanislaw want to take a walk by the ocean.

Mrs. Siezmagraff What a lovely idea, thank you, Buck. Mr. Vanislaw, you want to take a lovely walk? By the beach?

Mr. Vanislaw I can air my penis.

Mrs. Siezmagraff Well, yes, if it needs airing. (*laughs*) My, you're quite a handful. Trudy, dear, don't wait up. Who knows when we'll be back.

31

Mrs. Siezmagraff and Mr. Vanislaw exit merrily out to the deck and the beach beyond.

Buck I'm horny. I'm gonna go to a singles bar and pick up some chicks.

Betty I thought you were going to do the dishes.

Buck No. You do 'em. I gotta get laid. Catch ya later.

Buck exits.

Betty and Trudy sit in silence for a second.

They look pleasantly at each other. Betty and Trudy feel something vaguely unpleasant has happened, but they can't presently remember what it was. After a bit:

Voices What did Keith say?

Betty What?

Voices Did he say . . . he cut off heads?

Betty I think so. Trudy, did you hear him say he cut off heads?

Trudy He said he was an abused child. I was an abused child too. I want to comfort him.

Goes to his door.

Keith, are you all right? Can I come in?

Keith (*off*) I'm busy now. Leave me alone, please.

Trudy He's so hard to have a relationship with.

Betty Trudy. He said he cut off heads.

LAUGHTER.

(*to ceiling*) I don't think that's funny.

Voices No, you're right. It's not funny. Sorry.

32

Betty Should we call the police?

Trudy No. Betty, he's in pain. Psychological pain.

Betty I don't know. I don't feel that sorry for him if he's cutting people's heads off.

Trudy Well, he probably has an irresistible urge.

Betty Mmmm. I suppose.

Trudy (*knocking on Keith's door*) Were you abused very badly, Keith? I'd love to hear about it. I mean, if you'd like to share it with someone.

Keith (*off*) I don't like to talk about it. I'm sorry I brought it up.

Trudy Well, it's not good to keep your emotions in, Keith.

Keith (*off*) Please, I'm fine.

Trudy Keith, I want to comfort you.

Keith opens his door.

Keith I know you're being nice, but I can't be around people for too much of a time, and that charades game your mother forced me to be around went on for *hours*. So please, let me be by myself.

Trudy Well, what are you doing in there all that time?

Keith Nothing. I'm playing with my collection.

Trudy What collection?

Keith Just various things I've collected.

Betty (*polite but worried*) Keith, what have you collected? Do you have body parts in your room?

Keith Well, I have two feet.

Betty Oh my God.

Keith I have two feet. On the end of my legs. They're standing inside the door, so I have two feet inside my room.

Enjoys his joke.

Betty Oh. Well, what's in your hatbox?

Keith Hats! Look, I can't talk anymore, I'm sorry, I have seizures if I talk to people for too long. You don't want me to have a seizure, do you?

Betty No. I guess not.

Trudy Well, if ever you want to talk, I'm here, Keith, okay?

Keith Yeah, yeah, yeah. Where's Mr. Vanislaw?

Trudy He's taking a walk with my mother.

Keith Well, if you see him, tell him he can come in my room later.

Keith closes the door.

Trudy How could he possibly like Mr. Vanislaw???

Betty Well . . . I think he's crazy.

Trudy Who? Mr. Vanislaw?

Betty Well, he's crazy too. But I think Keith is crazy. This summer share isn't turning out at all as I imagined.

Trudy Really? I sort of imagined it this way.

Betty You did?

Trudy Well, my mother always does something to cause trouble. I'm going to take some pills and go to sleep. Good night.

Trudy exits to her room.

LAUGHTER.

Voices That was so abrupt!

Betty Yes, it was abrupt. Well, I guess I should do the dishes. Although I did cook the dinner. But then no one else will do them if I don't.

Voices Don't do them if you don't want to.

Betty Well, I suppose I could go for a walk.

Voices That's a good idea. Go for a walk.

Betty All right. I will. See you later.

Betty leaves.

APPLAUSE. LAUGHTER. SIGH.

Pause. Silence.

Voices Nothing's happening right now.

Silence.

I'm getting bored.
Keith—do you want to come out and entertain us for a while?
Keith?
Well, he's hopeless.
Gosh, we're just staring at the furniture.
We're just staring.

Calling plaintively.

Somebody . . . somebody. . . .

Lights go out.

End Scene

The same, later. The house is dark.

Mrs. Siezmagraff and Mr. Vanislaw come stumbling in.

Mrs. Siezmagraff Sssssshhh! You'll wake everyone.

Turns on the lights.

Mr. Vanislaw I turn into a werewolf at three a.m.

Mrs. Siezmagraff Really. You know, I think I had too many margaritas. I think I have to lie down right away.

Mr. Vanislaw You feel light-headed? Do some jumping jacks.

Mrs. Siezmagraff No, Mr. Vanislaw, I need to rest just a moment. Oh dear. Excuse me, I just need to lie down.

Mrs. Siezmagraff lies down, passes out. Mr. Vanislaw looks at her.

Mr. Vanislaw Stupid cow. Can't hold her liquor.

Keith looks out of his room.

Keith Pssssss.

Mr. Vanislaw What is that?

Keith Pssssssss.

Mr. Vanislaw Someone pissing?

Keith (*shyly, kind of sweet*) Mr. Vanislaw . . . I'm awake if you wanted to come visit for a while.

Mr. Vanislaw No, I want a woman now.

Kicks the body of Mrs. Siezmagraff.

Wake up, cow. Uh, she's a drunk. She can't stay awake after seven margaritas. I can drink lighter fluid and it doesn't affect me.

LAUGHTER.

Keith Would you like to see more of my collection?

Mr. Vanislaw Which room is Betty in?

Keith Betty doesn't like you.

Mr. Vanislaw That's all right. I enjoy struggle. Which room is she in?

Keith I don't want to say.

Mr. Vanislaw Oh, go to bed, little boy, you're annoying. Betty, Betty!

Mr. Vanislaw goes off to Betty's room. Keith watches after him, disappointed; then goes back into his room, closes the door.

A second later Mr. Vanislaw comes out.

Mr. Vanislaw She's not there. Where is the cow woman's daughter? Oh, Trudy . . . Mr. Vanislaw is here.

Mr. Vanislaw goes into Trudy's room. Inside the room, she screams. Keith pokes his head out of his door.

Vocal sounds of struggle inside Trudy's room.

Keith Trudy, are you all right?

Trudy (*offstage*) Stop it! Help! Help!

Keith Trudy, should I get your mother?

Trudy's struggle continues, but her sounds are more muffled now.

Keith goes over to Mrs. Siezmagraff.

Keith Mrs. Siezmagraff. Mrs. Siezmagraff. Can you wake up? It's your daughter. I think something is happening to her. Mrs. Siezmagraff.

Mrs. Siezmagraff (*stirring*) Hello. Come in please. Oh my head. Good Lord.

Keith Mrs. Siezmagraff. I think Trudy needs you.

Mrs. Siezmagraff Oh, that child. What is it this time?

Keith I think Mr. Vanislaw is raping her.

Mrs. Siezmagraff Did Trudy tell you that? That girl thinks men are lusting after her continually, and between you and me, they're not.

Keith (*emphatic, trying to get through*) I think he's raping her *now*.

Mrs. Siezmagraff Well, where is he? I don't even see him.

Keith He's in her room.

Mrs. Siezmagraff Oh, for God's sake! Every time I get a husband or a boyfriend, Trudy's always after them. (*to Trudy's door*) I hope you're not boring Mr. Vanislaw, Trudy.

Mr. Vanislaw (*off*) She's not!

Keith Mrs. Siezmagraff . . . you're not getting it. Mr. Vanislaw is taking Trudy against her will. Should we do something???

Mrs. Siezmagraff Do something. Um. Yes, we should.

Knocks on Trudy's door.

Mr. Vanislaw, I think you should come out now. Trudy needs her sleep. Come on out, both of you.

Mr. Vanislaw (*off*) I'm almost finished!

Mrs. Siezmagraff Now, I'm not kidding you two.

Mr. Vanislaw starts to make orgasm sounds. Mrs. Siezmagraff looks appalled.

Goodness. Well, now I'm getting annoyed.

Knocks on Trudy's door.

Stop that in there!

Mr. Vanislaw comes to the door, doing up his raincoat.

Mr. Vanislaw What, what? I thought you were passed out.

Mrs. Siezmagraff Keith woke me.

Mr. Vanislaw So now you're awake, what do you want?

Mrs. Siezmagraff Well, I hope you weren't forcing yourself on Trudy.

Mr. Vanislaw Every woman likes me. No need for forcing. I need a nap. Where can I sleep?

Mrs. Siezmagraff (*flirtatious*) Well, Mr. Vanislaw, I assumed you were going to stay with me.

Mr. Vanislaw I need rest. I can't have you groping me all night.

Keith You can sleep in my room.

Mr. Vanislaw I'll rest in the boy's room. I like the things in his room. Good night, see you in the morning.

Mr. Vanislaw goes off into Keith's room.

Mrs. Siezmagraff looks depressed and disappointed.

Mrs. Siezmagraff Oh, Lord, this evening is turning out terribly. (*pauses; to the ceiling*) I thought I'd hear laughter after that.

Voices We're very disturbed. We're not sure we feel like laughter.

Mrs. Siezmagraff Well, me neither.

Keith I hope Trudy is all right.

Mrs. Siezmagraff Well, she's been through worse things. I'm sure she's fine.

Keith (*nods; starts to think of having God knows what fun in his room; happy*) Well, good night.

Keith goes off to his room.

Mrs. Siezmagraff at rest for a moment, blank. Suddenly feels guilty about what Trudy's been through. Creeps up to her door.

Mrs. Siezmagraff (*outside Trudy's door; knocks lightly*) Trudy, dear, it's Mother. Are you all right? Should I come in? Do you want hot cocoa?

Trudy comes storming out, in T-shirt and shorts or underwear, wrapped in a summer blanket. Mrs. Siezmagraff jumps back, startled.

Trudy (*genuinely furious*) Why didn't you call the police????

Mrs. Siezmagraff What for?

Trudy That horrible man was raping me!

Mrs. Siezmagraff I hate all this date rape talk.

Trudy This was not date rape. You brought a maniac degenerate into the house, and he raped me while you did nothing.

Mrs. Siezmagraff (*angry*) I drank *seven* margaritas! Do you think I can be expected to be conscious after I drink seven margaritas!!????

Trudy Oh, well, in that case, no, just do nothing, it's perfectly understandable. Just like with my father for six years!!!

Mrs. Siezmagraff Your father is dead, Trudy. Must you insist on speaking against your poor father after he's dead??

Trudy I hate you. And I hate my father. And I hate that man. Where is he?

Mrs. Siezmagraff He's with Keith. And I must say I don't understand what the hell they could be doing.

Trudy goes to the kitchen, gets a large kitchen knife, and goes off into Keith's room.

Trudy. Be nice now.

From inside Keith's room, a terrible scream. From a man's voice. Mrs. Siezmagraff looks quizzical, decides it's probably nothing.

Brief pause. Keith comes charging out of his room.

Keith You better call the police.

Mrs. Siezmagraff Again? I can't keep calling the police! They'll think I'm a crank.

Trudy comes stumbling out of the bedroom, carrying something we can't quite see in her upstage hand.

Trudy (*hands it to her mother*) Here. You take it. I don't want it.

Mrs. Siezmagraff What is it?

Stares at it; it's vaguely sausagelike, but we don't get a clear view of it.

I don't understand. What is it?

Voices It's his penis, stupid.

Mrs. Siezmagraff looks horrified. Starts to move toward bedroom, then toward phone, then toward kitchen—an emotional overload of choices, what to do next.

Mrs. Siezmagraff Oh my God. We've got to call an ambulance. Keith, put this on ice. We've got to get doctors to sew this back on.

Trudy I don't want doctors to sew this back on. Give it to me, I'll throw it in the ocean.

Trudy grabs it back from her mother, and heads toward deck. Mrs. Siezmagraff stops her.

41

Mrs. Siezmagraff Trudy, if you throw that man's penis in the ocean, we won't be able to find it. How would you like it if someone cut your breast off and threw it in the ocean? Would you like that?

Trudy He raped me!

Trudy shakes the disconnected member at her mother, for emphasis. Perhaps the one and only time we see it clearly.

Keith goes back into his bedroom.

Mrs. Siezmagraff Well, even if he did, it wasn't irreparable. I mean, what you've done is a big overreaction.

Mrs. Siezmagraff grabs the member back from Trudy and goes toward the refrigerator.

Trudy Where are you going?

Mrs. Siezmagraff I'm putting this on ice.

Opens the freezer door, puts the member in the freezer, closes freezer door.

Trudy I don't want it in my refrigerator.

Mrs. Siezmagraff It's not your refrigerator. It's my house. I own it. Now stop acting like a spoiled brat. Oh, I better call an ambulance.

Picks up phone, speaks into it with intensity.

Hello. 911? 911?? Is anybody there???

Trudy You have to dial, Mother. You can't just pick up the phone and expect them to be there.

Mrs. Siezmagraff I did dial.

Dials for the first time.

Hello? Is this 911? There's an emergency here, we need help, a man has lost his penis and I have it in the refrigerator, and I wonder if there's anyone you know of who can sew it back on. (*listens*) No, I didn't do it. I'm not a maniac. It was my daughter. (*listens*) I don't know if he's conscious. Wait, I'll go see.

Mrs. Siezmagraff puts the phone down and goes into the bedroom. Trudy stays seated on the couch, sulky and chastised.

Pause. Mrs. Siezmagraff screams from offstage. Then comes running out.

Where is his head? What did you do with his head?

Trudy I didn't do anything to his head.

Mrs. Siezmagraff Well, he's headless. They're going to have to sew back his penis and his head, or else he's going to be totally useless. If we can even find the head.

Moves back toward the phone.

Trudy You can't sew a head back on, Mother.

Mrs. Siezmagraff I invite a guest into this house, and this is how he is treated. It's a disgrace. (*into the phone*) Forget the whole thing. He's been beheaded. There's no point in reattaching his penis anymore.

Hangs up.

I don't think, anyway.

Keith comes out of his room. He's not especially bloody, but is now wearing Mr. Vanislaw's raincoat.

Keith He hurt Trudy. Trudy's an abused child like me.

Trudy looks at Keith gratefully, with love.

Mrs. Siezmagraff Abused child. You're both spoiled brats.

Trudy Mother, he raped me.

Mrs. Siezmagraff Well, fine. File a report with the police. But don't cut off his penis. And, you, Keith, I assume it was you who cut off his head. Was that necessary?

Keith (*considers question*) Necessary? I don't know if it was necessary. Maybe.

The phone rings. Everyone looks at it. Mrs. Siezmagraff seems horrified, can't imagine why it should ring or who it could be. She goes back to the phone and answers it.

Mrs. Siezmagraff Hello? What? Well, I hung up because he's dead now, I assume. You can't live with your head cut off, can you? Oh, please, do we have to involve the police in it? The people who cut his head off didn't mean to. Well, it was an accident. I don't know how. Here, you speak to them.

She hands the phone brusquely to Trudy, and goes to fix herself a drink from a table or shelf with liquor bottles on it.

Trudy (*into phone*) Hello. What? My name is Trudy. What? Yes, I did. Why? Ummmm . . . it was in self-defense. No, I didn't cut his head off. Keith did. Well, it was in self-defense too. Uh-huh. (*listens*) Well, can't we just discuss it in the morning? Now? We have to go to the police station now? Well, it's awfully late. All right. All right.

Hangs up.

The woman at 911 says we have to go to the police station.

Mrs. Siezmagraff Trudy, I don't know why you can't leave well enough alone. Come on, let's go, but I hope this won't take all night.

Trudy gets a coat from her room, or slips into shorts or something. Mrs. Siezmagraff gulps down her drink, and then she, Trudy, and Keith leave by the upstage door, heading out to the driveway.

44

As they exit, LAUGHTER from the ceiling. Mrs. Siezmagraff stares up at it, alarmed as if the house is haunted; and they all three make their exit.

Pause. More LAUGHTER. Then SCREAMS. Then VOMITING sounds. Then sounds stop and they speak.

Voices We feel sick. We wish we were watching *The Waltons.*

Brief pause.

Enter Betty, seeming relaxed.

Betty Well, I feel much better after my walk.

Voices Uh-oh.

Betty Did you say "uh-oh"?

Voices No, we didn't say anything. Pay no attention to us.

Betty looks suspicious. Starts to look around the empty cottage.

Betty Is anyone here?

She notices that the door to Keith's room is wide open, which is unusual. Betty goes toward it.

Keith?

Betty goes into Keith's room.

From offstage, she screams hysterically. She comes running out. Screams some more. Goes to the phone, dials. Forgets how to talk, screams into the phone. Screams again. Then listens.

What? There's a body. Or part of a body. All bloody. I don't know where its head is. What? You know? What do you mean, you know? (*listens*) Oh, someone already spoke to you from here. Uh-huh. All right. Well, what should I do? Just sit tight. All right. I will. Yes. Thank you.

Betty hangs up, sits down, sits still, staring straight out. Screams again. And/or cries a bit. Can't seem to figure out how to get through the next minutes.

Oh God. (*pause*) I need a drink.

Betty goes to the table or shelf where the liquor is, grabs a big bottle of vodka. Pours herself a good stiff drink. Comes back to the couch. Sips her drink. It's awfully strong. And warm.

Oh. I need ice cubes. I knew something felt wrong.

Betty goes to the refrigerator, opens the freezer, looks in, screams hysterically . . . bolts backward into the room, dropping her glass, falling onto the floor.

LAUGHTER. APPLAUSE from the ceiling.

Blackout.

END ACT I

ACT TWO

The living room, a short time after previous scene. Betty is on the phone.

Betty Mother, it's me. Well, not very well actually. No, I'm not married yet. Yes, there are two men here, but I don't think either one of them is a likely candidate. Well, I can't say why, Mother, but just trust me. (*listens with irritation*) Fine, fine . . . I'll marry one of them. Do you want me to marry the macho pig or the serial killer? Well, I don't know how much they make a year. (*listens*) Mother, I called you because I was upset, but I think I'm going to hang up now. Never mind why I called. Well, there's a headless body in the bedroom and a penis in the refrigerator.

Pause.

Mother, are you there? Well, yes, the two things are connected. Or rather, they were connected, but Keith or someone cut the body parts off. Well, I don't know why, that's just the sort of thing Keith does, Mother. Well, Mrs. Siezmagraff chose him, I didn't. Well, no, the other one isn't nicer. On some level I prefer Keith.

Voices Get off the phone now, we want another scene.

Betty Mother, the voices want me to get off the phone now. The voices. I'm not *hearing* voices, mother. There *are* voices.

Holds phone up toward ceiling.

Say something.

47

Voices We love to laugh.

They laugh.

Ahahahahahahahahahahahahahahaha.

Betty See? They said they love to laugh. Well, I don't know. Ever since we got here. Mother, they're just a fact, I can't stop them. Uh-huh. Uh-huh.

Voices Get off the phone.

Betty I have to go now, Mother. I'll probably leave here tomorrow. Uh-huh. Uh-huh. Well, I'll try to get married, but I have to marry someone specific, don't I? Well, Daddy was specific, wasn't he? He wasn't? He was generic. In what way was Daddy generic? (*listens*) Uh-huh. Uh-huh. This is a longer conversation, Mother, and Daddy's not alive to defend himself.

Voices How did he die?

Betty (*answering them*) He died of a heart attack.

Voices Oh!

Laugh merrily.

Betty (*looks confused by Voices' response; then to phone*) No, Mother, I didn't laugh. Yes, and I know you know he died, I wasn't talking to you, I was talking to the Voices. (*listens*) I wasn't in the sun today, Mother. Never mind, forget it, good-bye, good-bye.

Hangs up.

Voices Entertain us, please.

Betty What?

Voices Entertain us.

Betty What should I do?

Voices Go to the refrigerator and look at the penis again.

Betty I don't want to.

Voices Please.

Betty No, I don't want to.

Voices Pleeeeeeeeeeeeeease.

Betty Oh, all right!

Voices (*excited*) Oooooooooooh!!!

Betty (*going to refrigerator*) This is so stupid.

Voices Open the freezer door.

Betty opens the freezer door, looks, runs to the sink, and vomits.

Betty (*into sink*) Blllllllllllllleeeeeeeeeeeehhhhhhhh.

Voices (*pleased*) Oooooooooooh! Yeah!

Sound of applause from the Voices.

Enter Buck.

Buck Someone applauding for me?

Betty No, it was for me.

Buck Oh yeah? What did you do?

Betty I threw up.

Buck Too much beer, huh? Grody.

Betty Yeah.

Buck I just balled two chicks on the beach, I think I got jism left for one more. You in the mood?

Betty I'm sick.

Buck Wanna feel my dick?

Voices (*delighted*) Oooooooooooh!

Sound of LAUGHTER and APPLAUSE. Buck looks appreciative.

Betty (*to Voices*) Shut up! Shut up!

Buck What are you so upset about?

Betty Doesn't it bother you, there are all these people in the ceiling?

Buck Are they in the ceiling?

Betty Or in the air. I don't know where they are. But don't they bother you?

Buck No, I like them. They like me. I feel approval.

Voices We do like you. We intend to nominate you for a People's Choice Award.

Buck (*very happy*) Cool. Thanks, guys.

Voices Hey, Buck. Why don't you make yourself a drink and put some ice cubes in it?

Buck Huh?

Voices Make yourself a drink.

Buck Okay.

Buck goes to the refrigerator, gets himself a beer.

I think I could do with a brew.

Voices (*very disappointed sound*) Ohhhhhhhhh.

Buck What's the matter?

Voices We want you to get ice cubes from the freezer.

Buck Ice cubes for my beer?

Betty (*with a touch of malice*) Why don't you have a vodka tonic or something?

Buck I like beer.

Voices She's right. Have a vodka.

Buck I don't like vodka.

Voices Please, please, please. . . .

Buck All right, all right. (*to Betty*) You're right, they are kind of annoying.

Pours himself vodka in a glass.

Vodka tonic. Vodka's a drink for businessmen. I'm a surfer dude, I like beer. Or tequila with worms in it.

Voices Stop complaining. Now get yourself some ice.

Buck Okay, okay.

Buck opens the freezer.

Voices (*excited anticipation*) Ooooooooh.

Buck, without really looking in, takes ice from the freezer quickly, plops it in his drink, and shuts the freezer door.

Buck There, I took some ice. Are you happy now?

Voices (*disappointed*) I guess so.

Buck Fuckin' hard-to-figure voices.

Voices There's something you didn't see in the freezer.

Buck Oh for Christ's sake.

With irritation he goes back to the freezer. Looks in. Uncertain initially what he sees.

What is that?

51

Sudden realization; screams in horror, slams freezer door shut.

Bummer! Bummer!

Voices Oooooooooo-weeeeeeee! That was fun!

Buck Whose is that?

Betty Mr. Vanislaw.

Buck What is this, some sort of chick revenge thing?

Betty I wasn't here when it happened. Do you want to see the headless body in the bedroom? I think that's Mr. Vanislaw too.

Buck No, I don't want to see the headless body. What's the matter with you?

Mrs. Siezmagraff comes back in, with Keith and Trudy.

Mrs. Siezmagraff We're back. And you should have heard the size of the bail we had to put up for these two. It's insane! People are just never presumed innocent in this country anymore.

Betty Innocent? There's a headless body in Keith's bedroom, and I found a penis in the refrigerator.

Mrs. Siezmagraff Yes, yes, we know this. No need to rub it in.

Trudy I don't feel well. Any chance I could be committed somewhere?

Mrs. Siezmagraff Darling, we'll hire you the best lawyers, I'm sure we can get you off.

Buck I'd like to get off.

Voices Why don't you sleep with Keith?

Buck Gross. He's another guy.

Keith I want to go to my room.

Mrs. Siezmagraff You can't go to your room. There's a body in there.

Voices We want to see Buck and Keith making out.

Buck Well, you're going to have to wait a long time then.

Mrs. Siezmagraff You know, Buck, if you were in a submarine for six months, I bet you'd start to think Keith was looking pretty good.

Buck No way, man.

Mrs. Siezmagraff Yes, way.

Betty This is really a side issue, isn't it? And I have a question. Why aren't the police here to remove the body, and look for clues, and all that?

Mrs. Siezmagraff They said they'd come here first thing tomorrow morning, and we weren't to touch anything.

Betty But it's a crime scene. They should be here.

Mrs. Siezmagraff Darling, this is a summer community, most of the police are in bed at this hour, or off committing adultery with Adelaide Marshall.

Buck Who's Adelaide Marshall?

Mrs. Siezmagraff She's the town randy widow.

Buck Cool. Where's the phone book?

Mrs. Siezmagraff (*points*) Over there.

Buck goes over to the table or shelf where the phone book is and starts paging through the M's.

Betty Well, I don't find this appropriate police behavior. If nothing else, they should come and remove the body.

Mrs. Siezmagraff I told you—they said they'd remove it in the morning.

Buck Got it!

Buck goes to the phone, dials.

Keith Well, if I can't stay in my room, I need to get some things out of there and put them in another room. And then I need to be able to shut the door. I can't be around people this long.

Trudy You can stay in my room, Keith.

Keith But you're a girl, it wouldn't be proper. Maybe I should stay in Buck's room, like the voices said.

Voices That's a good idea. We'd like to see Keith getting fucked by Buck. We're bored.

Buck Be quiet! (*into phone*) Hello, Adelaide. This is Buck. Are you there? Pick up if you're there. Well, maybe you're having group sex with the police. But I wanna leave you my number. 555-6822. I'm a real sexy guy, and I think you'd have a good time, baby.

Voices Ask her to come over, and then we can watch you, Keith, and Adelaide all together.

Buck hangs up phone.

Trudy Why don't the voices want to watch me have sex?

Voices You have a disturbing quality to you. So you don't trigger our erotic imaginations.

Trudy And you think Keith isn't disturbing?

Voices We find him very disturbing, but he's also strangely sweet. We plan to nominate him for a People's Choice Award.

Keith is initially pleased and a bit surprised at what the voices say. Though then he starts to feel uncomfortable as well.

Keith All this attention is making my head throb.

Voices (*kind of whispered*) Why don't you kill someone then?

Keith That's an idea.

Betty Stop, stop! (*strong, clearheaded*) The voices are talking too much. It's fine if they want to laugh from time to time—well, it's not fine, but I'm oddly used to it. But enough of this urging sex and murder. We've had enough for one day. Life has to have some dignity too, it's not all disgusting and vicious.

Voices She's right. Betty is right.

They give her a big round of applause. Betty is surprised by their reaction, and also oddly flattered.

Congratulations, Betty. You have appealed to our higher natures. We are ashamed of how we behaved a few minutes ago. But you are the voice of reason. You are the sort of person for whom *The Waltons* or *Touched by an Angel* is produced and aired. From now on, we will be good people. We love Betty! We send you kisses, Betty. Listen.

The Voices make nonsalacious kissing sounds. Betty is very flattered, smiles, is won over by all the praise.

Betty Well, thank you very much.

Pause; feels she's expected to say something else.

I just feel that people do have aspirations to higher things, to decent living, and I just felt the need to remind everyone of that.

Mrs. Siezmagraff Yeah, thanks a lot, we enjoyed it.

Trudy I feel ashamed. I wish I hadn't cut his penis off.

Keith I wish I were a fetus, and hadn't been born yet.

Buck I wish I was getting a blow job.

Voices Oh, Buck, you're so much fun! Betty, give him a blow job!

Betty What???

Voices We enjoy how honest Buck is. He's so horny. Why don't you give him a blow job?

Betty I thought you wanted to aspire to higher things.

Voices She's a prude. Why don't you take her in the other room and rape her, Buck? Rape Keith and Betty both. But videotape it because we want to watch it over and over.

Betty I have to leave this house!

Mrs. Siezmagraff Look, Betty, if you keep overreacting to every little thing that happens in life, then you're going to grow up just like my worthless daughter, Trudy. You've got to learn how to have fun in life. I like to go, go, go! It's like Auntie Mame said—life is a banquet, and most poor suckers are starving to death. But me, I stuff myself at the banquet—I stuff my mouth full of shrimp and chopped liver and pastries and champagne, and I mush it all up and I ram it down my throat because I want to live, live, live!

The Voices applaud.

Voices Bravo, Mrs. Siezmagraff. You have the most wisdom. You offer a life-is-fun philosophy that is very life-affirming. We love you, Mrs. Siezmagraff. Auntie Mame, Zorba the Greek, and now Mrs. Siezmagraff. We plan to nominate you for a People's Choice Award.

Mrs. Siezmagraff is very flattered and pleased with their reaction.

Trudy I seem to be the only one not nominated for a People's Choice Award.

Betty I'm not nominated for a People's Choice Award.

Mrs. Siezmagraff Well, what should we do next? Canasta? Yahtzee? Strip poker?

Trudy I don't want to play strip poker.

Keith Neither do I.

Mrs. Siezmagraff Oh, the young people nowadays. Big bores.

Voices Oh, the phone's going to ring.

They all look at the phone. It rings. Mrs. Siezmagraff is impressed. Goes to phone.

Mrs. Siezmagraff Hello? Who is this? Oh. Yes, he is. Hold on.

Hands phone to Buck.

It's Adelaide.

Buck (*very happy*) Hey, doll. How's it hangin'? Yeah? How many men? How big was the biggest one? Baby, I got him beat by a mile.

Trudy Well, hardly a mile, I've seen pictures.

Keith You have?

Buck (*to Trudy and Keith*) Ssssh! (*back to phone*) Yeah. Cool. What's your address. Uh-huh. Uh-huh. You got it, babe. What? Uh, I doubt it—but I'll ask. (*away from the phone*) Hey, Keith, you wanna meet a foxy lady?

Keith No, thank you.

Buck (*back into phone*) Sorry, babe. Well, I'll see if I can pick up any hitchhikers. Cool. Okay, babe. I'm comin' over. And then ... I'm comin'.

Hangs up.

Thank God she called back. I have so much testosterone if I don't come twenty times a day my brain gets soggy. See ya later!

Voices Don't go, Buck!

Buck Sorry, guys, gotta! I'll be back for my shut-eye!

Buck exits.

Mrs. Siezmagraff Well, I must say, I feel a little offended. We've all been through a trying time tonight, but I feel as a group we should stick together, and not go running off.

Trudy Well, you told him about the randy widow, didn't you?

Mrs. Siezmagraff Oh, shut up, Trudy.

Keith I have to go to bed now. My head hurts.

Mrs. Siezmagraff No, let's play a game. Or tell camp stories and roast marshmallows. Betty, you haven't had it that hard today, want to stay up and keep me company, and let the two psychos go to bed?

Betty No, thank you, Mrs. Siezmagraff, I don't want to roast marshmallows with you. I, for one, want to go to bed and forget everything about this horrible day; and then when the police come tomorrow, I'm getting a bus schedule and I'm leaving here.

Keith I need to lie down somewhere in quiet. Can't I just use my own room? I promise not to cut the body up.

Mrs. Siezmagraff Oh, do what you want to it, I don't care. I'm in a bad mood suddenly, I need to sleep too. Trudy, go to your room! If you hadn't overreacted to Mr. Vanislaw, this whole miserable thing wouldn't have happened.

Trudy I hate you! I wish you were dead!

Trudy runs off to her room. Keith starts to go to his room, and stops.

Keith You know, maybe I should stay in Buck's room tonight. I mean, so I don't do anything with the body.

Mrs. Siezmagraff (*temper tantrum*) I don't care what any of you people do! The younger generation is lacking in gratitude and joie de vivre. Fuck you and all your hatboxes!

Mrs. Siezmagraff storms off to her room.

Keith Do you think Buck will be angry if he finds me in his room?

Betty I don't know, Keith. I'm going to take a bath. I feel dirty.

Voices You look dirty.

Laugh.

Betty (*to Voices*) Fuck you, fuck you, fuck you. (*to herself*) To hell with my bath, I want to be unconscious right now!

She exits off to her bedroom, slams the door.

Keith I've gotta rest. I don't think Buck will mind. (*to Voices*) Good night.

Keith exits to Buck's room. Maybe turns the lights out.

Nothing happens for a while.

Voices Well, gosh. I didn't think they were really going to bed. Oh, people! Entertain us, please. Time to look in the freezer again. Or just come out and bicker in front of us again, and exchange insults. We love insult comedy. Entertain us, someone! Betty! Betty! Oh, Betty!

There is quiet for a little bit.

Bored; like children wanting to annoy, they do rhythmic nonsense syllables, kind of like saying "blah blah blah" in rhythm.

La da-da da-da da-da. La da-da da-da da-da. A-wooga! A-wooga! Fuck a duck, fuck a duck! Vomit, vomit. *Entertainment Tonight!* Tell us what Gwyneth Paltrow is doing *right this minute*! Come back, entertain us!!!

Betty comes tearing out of her bedroom. She is wearing a simple nightgown.

Betty Shut up!!! I need desperately to sleep. If you don't shut up, I'm going to go sleep on a sand dune.

Terrible sounds of ripping. A piece of the ceiling rips open—or a piece of the wall.

And out of this opening come Three People, all joined together.

They are the Voices—or at least three of them—who have crashed through the ceiling. They usually speak in unison.

They don't quite look like people—they are an "entity" together, they are joined at the hip by tubing like from a washing machine. This tubing is flexible and lets them move and stretch away from one another, but they none-theless stay always connected.

Or they might all three be connected to one lower body wrapped in black stretch fabric, say, with their six feet coming out the bottom. Like a three-headed being.

Coming out of the tops or sides of their heads are pieces of tubing with bits of wiring coming out of them, as if they had been living somehow inside the ceiling of the cottage, connected to wires and tubing and God knows what else.

But they have now ripped themselves out of that situation due to the need to confront the people who have so rudely gone to bed and left them with nothing to watch.

On their feet there may be large garbage bags tied as enormous shoes.

Though meant to be one "entity," their faces do express their individuality. And there are three faces and three voices, those of a man, a woman, and another man.

VOICE 1 is male, a bit sensitive, chatty, enthusiastic. VOICE 2 is female, articulate, together, sometimes charming. VOICE 3 is male, a bit macho, capable of anger and being a bully. And all three of them can get ferocious when they're dissatisfied. Presently they're feeling ferocious.

The Voices are the laugh track of the house, but now they have shown up in person.

Betty screams when she sees them.

Voices ENTERTAIN US!

Betty Help! Mrs. Siezmagraff!

Voices Look in the freezer again!

Due to the noise of the figures crashing through the ceiling, Mrs. Siezmagraff, Trudy, and Keith all come charging out of their rooms—and are frightened and confused by what they see. Trudy and Keith are dressed for bed. Mrs. Siezmagraff has not changed clothes yet. Betty or Keith turns the lights back on, so we and they get a better look at them.

Voices Make us laugh. Gross us out. Tell us the latest news of Gwyneth Paltrow. Show us naked pictures of Brad Pitt! Vomit in the sink! Entertain us! Waaaaa-aaaaaaaaa!

The Voices start to cry—I Love Lucy-"Waaaaa" style—at their frustration at not being entertained.

Trudy Oh my god, what is it?

Betty They came from the ceiling.

Voice 1 (*male*) That's a good title. "They Came From the Ceiling."

Betty Who are you?

Mrs. Siezmagraff Do you play charades?

Voice 2 (*female*) No, thank you. We prefer to watch.

Voices ENTERTAIN US!

Keith (*feels he should oblige them; sings shyly*)
Me and my shadow,
Strolling down the avenue,
Me and my shadow. . . .

Betty (*to Keith*) Stop it! I don't know what's happening.

Voices We are so intrigued by the case of the headless body with the penis in the refrigerator. We want this case to go on Court TV.

Mrs. Siezmagraff Oh, what a good idea. And Trudy darling, we'll hire a marvelous attorney who can get you off.

Voices We can't wait that long. We want the trial now.

Mrs. Siezmagraff But it's the middle of the night.

Voices Now. Gratify us now.

Mrs. Siezmagraff They're so demanding.

Voices Now, now! Court TV now!

Mrs. Siezmagraff (*suddenly oddly willing*) All right.

Betty Wait a minute. Who are these creatures? Are they aliens? Should we call the police?

Mrs. Siezmagraff We can't keep calling the police every time some little thing happens. I mean we're used to hearing them laugh all day long, now they've just shown up in person.

Voices Mrs. Siezmagraff, you are filled with wisdom. We love you!

Mrs. Siezmagraff Well, thank you. Now how shall we begin the trial?

Betty Well, it won't be binding. There's no judge, no jury, it's not a real trial.

Voice 3 (*male; angry, nasty*) We know that, Betty! But it will be good practice for the real Court TV trial. And you'd all gone to bed and we had nothing to look at!

Betty Okay, okay. Don't be mad.

Voice 3 Fucking cunt!

Voice 2 (*smiles, charming; she's kind of articulate and pleasant much of the time*) But we don't want to offend you. We just want a little taste of what the case will be like on Court TV.

Voice 1 (*chatty, enthusiastic; he's not macho*) We think it has great potential. We loved the Lorena Bobbitt case. We loved both cases, his and hers, and how juries found both of them innocent. In her trial, she seemed very sweet, like when she cut off his penis, she was just pushed too far, and he was abusive and horrible! And then in his case, he seemed falsely accused, she seemed like a real maniac. And so both of them got off, it was very amusing!

All three of them laugh.

It was a real exercise in switching your point of view.

Voice 2 It really held our attention. And we were thrilled when several months later Lorena Bobbitt was arrested for beating up her mother! She constantly holds our attention.

Voice 3 We're angry that Andrew Cunanan died and didn't have a trial on television. We weren't ready for his story to be over. We wanted a few more killings and then a long, disgusting trial. We're angry that Michael Jackson's child molestation case was settled out of court. We wanted it on television. We wanted *months and months* of humiliating, degrading revelations. We wanted to know if his penis is discolored or not. Is it? Is it?

Mrs. Siezmagraff I'm sure I don't know.

The Three Figures Begin the trial, please.

> *Loud Court TV-like music starts . . . pulsating, rhythmic, like the music that introduces the evening news or that introduces repeated news coverage of things with titles like "Crisis in the White House" or "President Under Fire."*
>
> *The Voices disengage from any wires that helped them lower themselves into the room, and send the wires back up; and the ceiling closes up.*
>
> *Meanwhile, downstage of them, Mrs. Siezmagraff confers in whispers with Trudy and Keith on courtroom strategy. Keith seems resistant about something, and Mrs. Siezmagraff hits Keith on the arm or shoulder a number of times. Trudy doesn't like that.*
>
> *Also, at Mrs. Siezmagraff's instructions, Keith and Trudy move furniture around to get ready for the trial: The couch is moved so it is in the best place to be a jury box; and a chair is moved so it can be the witness chair.*
>
> *The music finishes, and the Voices sit on the couch.*

Mrs. Siezmagraff (*finishing up any furniture adjustments to set up for the trial*) I don't know which one of us should be Leslie Abramson. Betty, do you want to be?

Betty I don't want anything to do with this.

Mrs. Siezmagraff Well, it seems to me I'll have to be the defense attorney and defend my darling daughter, Trudy, who's been so wronged, and her interesting, disturbed friend Keith, who if one of them has to be punished, I think I'll sacrifice him.

Keith looks worried, but then goes and sits on the side, out of the way.

Now. My first witness is Trudy Siezmagraff, accused of malicious assault and removing of genitals.

Trudy sits in the witness chair. Mrs. Siezmagraff stands by her.

How do you plead?

Trudy He raped me.

Mrs. Siezmagraff No, no, that's not a plea. Guilty or not guilty.

Trudy Guilty.

Mrs. Siezmagraff No, dear. We never say guilty. We say not guilty.

Trudy Well, I did cut his penis off, didn't I?

Mrs. Siezmagraff Darling, it's not your fault. He was raping you. And that was traumatizing. And you were also raped by your father, and both times your mother didn't help you or aid you, and you just had no choice except to cut his penis off. I mean, you did it as a statement, right?

Trudy Yes. It was a statement.

Looks over and checks to see how the jury/Voices like this tack.

Mrs. Siezmagraff You didn't mean it to be irreparable. You intended that it would be sewn back on. Then it would have been fine, just like with Mr. Bobbitt, and he could have even made some pornographic films like Mr. Bobbitt. Right?

Trudy That's right. I wanted to teach him a lesson, but I knew they could sew his penis back on.

Voices We liked that pornographic movie showing John Bobbitt having sex. We're angry Tom Cruise doesn't show his penis!

Betty You know, if I counted the number of times I have heard the word "penis" used today, I could . . . well, I don't know what.

Mrs. Siezmagraff I'm sorry, are you speaking as the prosecuting attorney, or as Betty?

Betty Well, Betty.

Mrs. Siezmagraff Well, we don't need to hear from Betty right now.

Trudy I'm not guilty. It was an impulse. I thought it could be put back on. I'm not responsible because I had a traumatic childhood.

Voices 1 & 2 Poor Trudy. We feel sorry for her.

Voice 3 Bitch, cutting off his dick.

Voice 2 (*angry, passionate*) She was raped. She was upset. She took a knife and did what any normal woman would do.

Betty I object.

Voice 2 Well, fuck you!

Betty (*strong, clearheaded again*) I just have to go on record saying I don't believe you are allowed to do anything you want just because you're upset, or you had a bad childhood. I don't mean to minimize the rape—that is terrible, but there are police and courts and you just don't take justice into your own hands. Look at the lynching of blacks when that was done. Mob rule is a bad thing, whether it's done by a group of people or by one person. Trudy, I know it was awful, but you didn't have a right to do what you did. And Keith, you really didn't have a right to do what you did. (*to everybody*) We have to agree not to harm one another. That's one of the basic rules of civilization.

Voices (*genuine; even teary*) We are so moved. You have spoken eloquently. We will now nominate you for a People's Choice Award, after all. You have once again appealed to our better nature.

Betty Well . . . thank you.

Voices (*harsh, angry*) Trudy, you have fallen from our favor. Betty has convinced us you are responsible for your actions. We want you to receive the death penalty, and we want to see you executed on television!

Voice 3 (*makes electric chair noise*) Bzzzzzz. Bzzzzzzzzz.

Voices 1 & 2 Kill her! Kill her! Kill the bitch!

Trudy (*crying, hysterical*) Oh my God, oh my God.

Mrs. Siezmagraff (*annoyed at Betty*) Oh, now look what you've done. (*to Trudy*) Don't worry, Trudy, Momma will save you.

> *Mrs. Siezmagraff begins to interrogate Trudy. Her voice doesn't change much from her usual voice, but her manner is more lawyerly. Simple, to the point—like a good no-nonsense lawyer on Court TV.*

Trudy, you had a horrible childhood, didn't you?

Trudy Yes, I did.

Mrs. Siezmagraff Your father molested you often, didn't he?

Trudy Yes, he did.

Mrs. Siezmagraff And what of your mother?

Trudy She did nothing. When I told her about it, she called me a liar and a seducer.

Mrs. Siezmagraff I call Mrs. Siezmagraff to the witness stand.

(calls out, as if she's the bailiff now as well)

Mrs. Siezmagraff! Mrs. Siezmagraff! Come to the witness stand.

(speaking as herself)

Coming!

(as bailiff, running the words together)

Do you swear to tell the truth, the whole truth, and nothing but the truth?

(as herself)

I do.

(as the lawyer again; she is the defense attorney, interrogating)

Mrs. Siezmagraff, you are the mother of the accused, are you not?

(as herself)

Yes, I am.

(as defense attorney)

May I say that you are looking especially lovely this evening?

(as herself; genuinely flattered)

Oh, thank you.

Voice 1 Objection!

Voice 2 Irrelevant!

Voice 3 Sustained!

Mrs. Siezmagraff (*annoyed; but moves on; now as defense attorney*) Mrs. Siezmagraff, did you know that your husband, Trudy's father, raped her repeatedly in her childhood?

(*as herself; angry; her eyes flash*)

Did she tell you that? She's a liar!

The Three Figures (*excited by the drama*) Ooooooooooh.

Trudy Momma, Momma.

Mrs. Siezmagraff (*as herself*) I have to tell the truth, Trudy.

(*as attorney*)

Mrs. Siezmagraff, is it not true that Trudy told you what was happening, and you refused to believe her?

(*as herself*)

She never told me. She never told me anything. I was a perfect mother. I don't know why she's telling these lies about me!

(*as attorney*)

I call to the stand Mrs. McGillicutty, your Irish housekeeper.

(*as herself; baffled*)

I never had a housekeeper. I don't know who you're talking about.

(*as attorney*)

Mrs. McGillicutty, you were in the employ of Mrs. Siezmagraff over there, were you not.

Now she's the Irish maid, speaking with a very pronounced Irish accent.

Oh, b'gosh and b'garin, yes, I worked for Mrs. Siezmagraff for many years.

(*as herself*)

That's a lie! She's a liar!

(*as attorney*)

Be quiet! Mrs. McGillicutty, can you prove to us that you worked for Mrs. Siezmagraff?

(*as Irish maid*)

Oh yes, m'lord. Here are my pay stubs for my work for five years.

(*as herself*)

Those are forgeries! I've never seen this woman before in my life!

(*as Irish maid*)

B'gosh and b'garin, Mrs. Siezmagraff, don't you recognize me? I'm Kathleen. I come all the way from Kilarney to be with your family and mind your little daughter, Trudy.

(*as herself; getting hysterical*)

I've never seen you. You're a liar! Listen to her accent. She's not really Irish.

(*as Irish maid; offended*)

I am Irish. And I worked for you for five years. Trudy remembers me, don't you, Trudy?

Trudy (*not quite certain what to say*) Yeah . . . I remember you.

Mrs. Siezmagraff (*as herself*) Trudy, you're lying!

(*as attorney*)

Don't be afraid of your mother, Trudy. Just tell the court the truth.

(*as Irish maid*)

Oh, Trudy. Remember you and I spent many a happy hour. I would read you stories about the leprechauns and the funny mischief they would do. You remember, don't you, Trudy?

Trudy Yes, Mrs. McGillicutty.

Mrs. Siezmagraff (*as attorney*) Mrs. McGillicutty. Did you ever see Trudy's father molest her?

(*as Irish maid*)

Yes, I did.

(*as herself*)

She's lying!

(*as attorney*)

And do you have any firsthand knowledge that Trudy's mother knew her husband was molesting Trudy?

(*as Irish maid*)

Yes, I do.

(*as herself; vicious and seething*)

That's not true! She's lying!

(*as attorney*)

Mrs. McGillicutty, what is the knowledge you have?

(*as Irish maid*)

On April fourth, 1978, Mrs. Siezmagraff said to me, "I know my husband is raping my daughter, but I don't want to say anything to him, because I'm afraid he'd leave me."

(*as herself*)

You Irish pig! You liar!

(*as Irish maid*)

And when she said that, I happened to be speaking into a tape recorder, making a transcription of my special Irish stew recipe, and so I have a recording of her admission on tape. So don't you be calling me a liar, Mrs. Siezmagraff. I'll take you to court and sue you for slander.

Mrs. Siezmagraff, caught by the Irish maid's evidence, now has full-fledged hysterics, and rushes center stage.

(*as herself; hysterics*)

It's true! It's true! I knew what was going on. And I didn't stop it. I was afraid I'd lose him. It's my fault Trudy was molested over and over and over, and no wonder she attacked Mr. Vanislaw. And I could've stopped Mr. Vanislaw's raping her, but I was drunk! I had had seven margaritas and I passed out.

Weeps.

I'm sorry, Trudy, I'm sorry—I ruined your life.

Trudy Momma, Momma!

Weeps.

Mrs. Siezmagraff (*crescendo: on her knees, out front*) Don't convict my daughter! It's my fault. I didn't protect her. It's my fault. CONVICT *ME*, CONVICT *ME*!

Collapses to the ground, weeps.

Trudy, weeping, embracing her mother. They hold each other and continue to weep.

The Voices are moved, dab their eyes, make sympathetic sounds.

Voices (*after a bit*) We are so moved.

Dab their eyes some more.

Mrs. Siezmagraff Trudy, Trudy.

Trudy Momma. Oh, Momma.

Voices We are moved out of our minds. We hereby acquit Trudy of all charges. Beloved Trudy, you are free. Go and live your life.

The Voices beam and smile warmly at Trudy and Mrs. Siezmagraff.

Trudy Oh, Momma, thank you. At last I have the mother I always wanted. And for everything you did in the past—I forgive you.

Mrs. Siezmagraff Well, it's about time.

Trudy What?

Mrs. Siezmagraff I'm just saying you took a long time to get to forgiveness. A lot of children would have gotten over it a long time ago and not gone ballistic when some man in a raincoat showed them some attention.

Trudy I hate you.

Moves far away from her mother; furious.

Mrs. Siezmagraff Well, your grateful period didn't last very long, did it?

Voices Now do Keith's trial.

Mrs. Siezmagraff Oh, God, I don't have the energy. Betty, can you do it?

Betty Ummmm . . . I'd rather not.

Mrs. Siezmagraff Look, I did the first one.

Voices Try it, Betty!

Betty Okay.

Mrs. Siezmagraff maybe gets herself a soda, and hangs out with the jury for a bit.

Betty stands by the witness chair, and Keith crosses to the chair, a bit pleased and excited at the attention he's about to get. He sits in the chair.

Um . . . Keith, you cut the man's head off, right?

Keith Yes.

Betty And you knew what you were doing when you did that, right?

Keith Yes.

Betty And you've killed other people too, right?

Mrs. Siezmagraff No, no, no, stop. This is not how to do a trial. Gosh, it's pointless trying to delegate authority, I always have to do everything myself.

Betty gives up and walks away. Mrs. Siezmagraff goes over to Keith in the witness chair.

Tries to do it fast.

Keith, you were molested, right? And treated really badly, right?

Keith Yes. I was. I was molested by twenty people.

The Voices are suitably and gruesomely impressed.

Mrs. Siezmagraff Well, you had quite a large family, didn't you? Or were some of those people neighbors? Never mind, we don't need to know.

Keith We had cousins from the Ozarks living with us. And they had all cross-pollinated.

Mrs. Siezmagraff Cross-pollinated. Please don't make this too interesting, we have to move through this quickly. So—Keith, you were molested by twenty people, and then you were criticized unrelentingly too, weren't you? "Keith, you're too slow." "Keith, you're stupid." "Keith, you're not man enough." "Keith, you're this, Keith, you're that." Am I right, Keith?

Keith Yes. That is right. All twenty members of my family said I was worthless.

Voices You are worthless.

Keith Yes, like that.

Mrs. Siezmagraff And Keith, right before you cut off Mr. Vanislaw's head, I bet he had been criticizing you, right?

Keith (*uncertain*) I'm not sure.

Mrs. Siezmagraff God, you're stupid. Keith, think harder. I think Mr. Vanislaw criticized you unrelentingly just like the members of your large family did. Is that right? Say yes.

Keith Yes, he did.

Mrs. Siezmagraff And I bet you thought that if he kept criticizing you that your head would explode, is that right, Keith? Say yes.

Keith Yes, that's right.

Mrs. Siezmagraff And so because you literally thought your head would explode, you *had* to kill Mr. Vanislaw, didn't you? And thus your action was actually in self-defense. Am I correct? Say yes.

Keith You're correct. I did it to defend myself.

Mrs. Siezmagraff You see! He's innocent, he's innocent.

Voices We see his pain. We hereby acquit him. Go and find happiness, beloved Keith. You are free.

Keith I'm free. I killed out of self-defense because I thought my head would explode.

Mrs. Siezmagraff (*a bit tired*) That's right, Keith.

Keith And also because I like to cut heads off.

Mrs. Siezmagraff and the jury/ Three Figures are taken aback by this comment.

Mrs. Siezmagraff You're a difficult client, Keith. We'll just take that last comment as kind of . . . a joke, I guess. Was it a joke, Keith?

Keith Yes, I have a quiet sense of humor.

Mrs. Siezmagraff Yes, you do. Your actions are loud and noisy, but your humor is quiet. Now can we stop Court TV for a while? All this strategy and planning has made my head hurt. I've got to lie down. I think I have some Twinkies in my room, my blood sugar is dropping. Excuse me. I need some sugar, and a nap.

Voices Wait! Give us some of your wonderful philosophy again before you leave.

Mrs. Siezmagraff (*not really in the mood*) Oh. Um. Life is great. Live, live, live. Eat food at the banquet . . . to life, to life, l'chaim!

Mrs. Siezmagraff stumbles/dances off to her room.

Trudy looks at Keith longingly.

Trudy Keith.

Keith Yes?

Trudy I love you.

Keith I love you too.

Voices Ahhhhhhhhh.

Trudy goes over to Keith and reaches out to touch him.

Keith (*recoils in fear*) Plese don't touch me.

Voices Uh-oh.

Trudy Okay. But someday I can touch you, can't I?

Keith I don't think so.

Trudy Life is so unhappy. I want to go to sleep now.

Keith Me too.

Betty Me three.

Voices NO!

Betty We're tired.

Trudy Keith, why don't you rest in my room? You don't want to be alone tonight, do you?

Keith I like to be alone.

Voices Don't go yet, please.

Trudy Well, Keith, I don't want to be alone. You can sleep on the whole other side of the room. I won't come near you, I promise. But I need company.

Voices We need company too.

Trudy Please, I'm exhausted. Keith, will you come with me?

Keith Oh, all right.

Voices Don't go.

Trudy (*cranky*) We're tired!

Trudy and Keith exit to Trudy's room.

Voices Well, we're *not* tired. Don't leave us. Betty, help us focus our minds on something.

Voice 1 I want to see naked pictures of Brad Pitt.

Voice 3 I want to see naked pictures of Cameron Diaz.

Voice 2 I want to see Hugh Grant in bed with a prostitute.

Voice 1 I want to see Clarence Thomas giving Anita Hill a Coke can with pubic hair on it.

Voice 3 That bitch, she lied!

Voice 2 She told the truth!

Voice 1 Clarence Thomas likes movies starring Long Dong Silver.

Voices We have that in common.

Happily listing things they love.

Sex. Murder. Mayhem. Human Interest Stories About Kittens. Kitty and Jose Menendez Served in a Casserole!

The Voices all look at Betty.

Betty Well, I do think it's rather late.

Betty tries to leave the room.

Voices (*screaming at her*) We're not done yet!

Betty Now, look!—you've had a sexual assault, a removal of genitals, a beheading, and a simulation of a very dramatic trial. I don't know what else you want from us.

The Voices whisper and confer.

Voices Do you have any of the *Naked Gun* movies on tape? O. J. Simpson is in them.

Betty No, we don't. Now, good night.

Voice 2 Wait! (*little girl*) Tell us a bedtime story, Betty. Please.

Voices Please, Betty. Please.

Betty All right. But then you've got to sleep.

Looking vaguely above her.

And maybe go back into the ceiling if you can.

Voices Soothe us. Sooooothe us.

The Voices sit back down on the couch and kind of cuddle together. They luxuriate in the pleasure of the bedtime story to come.

Betty All right. Once upon a time . . .

Voice 2 (*little girl-ish*) When?

Betty Long ago.

Voices (*sighing, satisfied*) Long ago.

Betty There lived a princess.

Voice 1 Ooooh, a princess. I want to wear a dress.

Voice 3 Faggot.

Voice 1 Butch heterosexual bully!

Voice 2 Please, please, she's telling us a story. Go on, Betty.

Betty I don't know what I'm talking about. Okay, there's this princess. And she has a curse on her.

Voice 1 Oooooo, menstruation.

The other two giggle.

Betty Stop it. That's childish.

The Voices look suitably chastised, and settle back down, like children told they've been bad.

A witch put a curse on the princess, that she had to find true love before eleven o'clock at night, or else . . . well, Or Else. And then at ten-forty-five the door bell of the castle rang, and in walked . . . seven dwarfs, and a gnome, and a person with a harelip.

Voice 2 This is starting to wake me up.

Voice 1 (*getting excited by his fantasy*) And the princess was really Andrew Cunanan in drag. And he killed all seven dwarfs, who were gay.

Voice 2 And the gnome collects shoes belonging to Marla Maples.

Voice 3 And the person with a harelip is an S&M dominatrix who bites Marv Albert on the buttocks.

Voice 1 And then Frank Gifford has sex with Tonya Harding while Kathie Lee watches.

Voice 2 (*terribly happy*) And Amy Fisher has sex with Joey Buttafuoco and Charles Manson and a pig! And they make three TV movies about it!

Voice 3 And then Buck comes home, and he's still horny, so he rapes Trudy and Keith.

Voice 1 Or maybe just Keith.

Voice 2 And then Trudy and Keith do it again.

Voices They cut off his penis and behead him!

Voice 1 That's Entertainment Part Two!

Voice 3 Oh Buck!

Voice 2 Buck!

Voices Oh, Buck! Buck! Buuuuuuu-uuuuuuuuck!

Enter Buck.

Buck Jeeze! That Adelaide was nothing but a cock tease. She never let me come, and now I'm so fuckin' horny my nuts hurt. You ever have your nuts hurt?

Voices We have an idea, Buck.

Betty No, Buck, go outside again. Hurry. (*to The Three Figures*) You said you were going to sleep. I'll do a better story. Once upon a time . . .

Voice 3 We're sorry you're horny, Buck.

Voice 1 Why don't you fuck Keith finally? It wouldn't be like you're gay. You're just horny.

Voice 2 You've only had sex twenty times today.

Betty No. Buck, run for your life. Don't stay here.

Buck (*to Betty*) What—ya jealous?

Voice 1 Fuck Keith.

Voice 3 It's okay with me, man. It don't mean nuthin'. Treat him like a pussy.

Voice 2 And tell Trudy she's not attractive enough, and you prefer Keith to her.

Buck Well . . . I do gotta get my rocks off.

Betty (*annoyed*) You haven't even seen them before. Don't you want to ask who they are?

Buck They're the people in the ceiling, right?

Betty (*disoriented by his acceptance*) Right.

Voices They're in Trudy's room, Buck. They're there together. They're waiting for you. Go take your pleasure, Buck.

Buck Yeah. Keith'll probably like it. Thanks, guys.

Calls out.

Oh, Keith. Trudy. Buck is home.

Betty Don't let him in!

Betty tries to hold Buck back, or to block the door. Buck easily pushes her aside. Keith opens the door.

Keith Oh, hi, Buck.

Buck Keith, my man. You're lookin' mighty good tonight.

Keith Oh really? Why don't you come in. Look, Trudy, look who's here.

Betty Don't go in there, Buck.

Buck goes into the room. They shut the door behind him.

Betty holds her hands over her ears. The Voices listen attentively, excited.

After a moment the sounds of terrible screams from Buck. Then more screams. During this, the Voices are delighted.

Voices Oooooooooh! Yeah. Go get 'im. Chop off his dick! Chop off his head! Oooooooooh. Chop him into hamburger!

The noises of Buck screaming stop.

Mrs. Siezmagraff comes charging out of her room.

Mrs. Siezmagraff What is going on here??? I'm trying to sleep, you selfish children!

Trudy comes out of the bedroom. She's wiping her bloody hands on a dish towel.

Trudy Mother. We've done it again.

Mrs. Siezmagraff Done what again?

Trudy You know. What we did earlier.

Mrs. Siezmagraff I don't understand what you're saying.

Trudy (*trying to explain; she doesn't quite understand what made them do it either*) Buck came back.

Mrs. Siezmagraff Oh my God.

Looks into the room.

Oh my God.

Voices Vomit in the sink! Vomit, vomit!

Keith, also a bit bloody, comes out of the room and stands next to Trudy.

Mrs. Siezmagraff What kind of behavior is this? Are you two just totally insane?

Trudy (*angry, firm*) Mother—we had very difficult childhoods.

Mrs. Siezmagraff Oh, "blah, blah, blah" your childhoods. I got a splinter once when I was three. Do you see me killing people?

Keith (*shouts for the first time*) That's an idiotic comparison, you cow!

Mrs. Siezmagraff (*shocked, but ignores his outburst*) Look, when I got you two acquitted of the charges, that was rehearsal, you know. That wasn't really Court TV. That was practice. I can't get you acquited if you've gone and done it again!

Trudy We weren't on Court TV?

Mrs. Siezmagraff No, Trudy. And no matter how pathetic we make you sound, no jury in their right mind is going to acquit you if you've cut off the penises and heads of *two people in one day.*

Trudy They will acquit us. We'll make them cry.

Mrs. Siezmagraff I don't think so. Goodness, Buck. He was a very nice person. Women like men who put out, Trudy—but you wouldn't know about that.

Keith Shut up, you cow!

Mrs. Siezmagraff Shut up yourself.

Trudy You mean I might go to prison?

Mrs. Siezmagraff Well, I would think so, Trudy.

Trudy (*pointing to The Three Figures*) They made us do it.

Mrs. Siezmagraff You really blame people a lot, don't you, Trudy?

Keith Don't you pick on Trudy, you cow, or I'll cut your head off.

Mrs. Siezmagraff Stop calling me a cow.

Keith Cow! Cut your head off!

Voices Cut her head off, cut her head off.

Betty (*ferocious*) STOP IT! NO MORE CUTTING OFF OF HEADS!!!

Voices Well . . . blow up the house then.

Keith That's a good idea. They're gonna give me the electric chair anyway. I'm tired of living.

Mrs. Siezmagraff (*trying to stop him*) Now, Keith . . .

Keith goes over to the kitchen area.

84

Keith This is a gas oven, isn't it?

Betty, unprepared for this, tries to appeal to Keith from time to time, saying "no" and "no, Keith"—but he's quite far gone now.

Trudy Good idea! Let's kill ourselves and Mother, and blow the house up.

Keith turns on the gas jets. Exaggerated sound of gas escaping.

Mrs. Siezmagraff No, Keith. I own this house. And I get rental income. We don't want to blow it up.

Trudy (*to the Voices*) Hold her!

The Voices grab on to Mrs. Siezmagraff and won't let her go.

Mrs. Siezmagraff Oh my God.

Voices Stay put, bitch.

Mrs. Siezmagraff I thought you liked me.

Voices We like you dead on toast.

Trudy (*emphatic; kind of happy*) Mother, it's all your fault. And Daddy's fault. And Keith's twenty relatives' fault. And Oliver Stone's fault for making *Natural Born Killers*. And now we're all going to die.

Mrs. Siezmagraff No, Trudy. Life is wonderful. It's great fun. Whee, wheee, wheeee!

Keith I've got the match ready.

Betty Keith, don't strike the match.

Keith But I want to.

Voices Betty, we allow you to escape. Hurry—run out of the house.

Betty But stop this from happening.

Voices You have ten seconds, Betty. One, two, three . . .

Trudy
Stay here, Betty.   And
die with us!

Voices
Four, five, six, seven . . .

Betty No. . . .

Voices Eight, nine . . .

Betty Good-bye!

Betty runs like crazy out of there—through the door to the deck and the beach and ocean beyond.

Voice 1 We're ready, Keith.

Voice 2 Light the match, Keith.

Voice 3 Blow it to fuckin' smithereens, baby!

Trudy (*closes the door Betty left by; looks at her mother, with an evil look*) Good-bye—Mrs. Siezmagraff.

Keith Here goes.

Keith lights the match.

Terrible flash. Sound of enormous explosions.

Blackout.

End Scene

SCENE TWO/EPILOGUE

The beach, moments later.

Betty comes running out, in her nightgown.

*It's dark on the beach. We hear the sounds of waves, and
we hear the sounds of explosions in the background. In the
distance, behind the dunes, we see a red and orange glow of
the house burning.*

*Betty is scared and out of breath. She looks back to where
the house burning is. Then out front again.*

Betty (*speedy, upset; to herself*) Where am I going to sleep
tonight? I don't know why the people in the ceiling let me
leave. I don't think I could have saved Mrs. Siezmagraff. I
don't feel too guilty about it. I mean, they all seemed really
terrible. I feel bad for Trudy, sort of . . . but well, I don't
know what to think.

*Looks out to the audience; includes them in her thoughts
now.*

Now, actually, I think I'd like to become a hermit. Or I might
become a nun if I could live in a convent in an isolated area
with no other people around, and where no one in the convent is allowed to speak *ever*. I'd like that if it was quiet,
and peaceful, and if they didn't care if I believed in God
or not.

Another idea.

Or maybe I could start my own community where people
don't speak. And we'd plant our own food, and we'd
watch the birds in the trees. And maybe I'm having a
breakdown.

Holds the sides of her head, as if it might fly apart.

Or is it a breakthrough?

Hopeful; another possibility.

Maybe it's a bad dream I had, and am still having.

Looks around her.

But I seem to be on the beach. And the house seems to be smoldering somewhere behind me in the distance.

Looks behind her; the glow is almost out now; the sound of explosions has stopped; we hear the sound of the ocean.

Isn't the sound of the ocean wonderful?

Calming down slightly.

What is it about it that sounds so wonderful? But it does. It makes me feel good. It makes me feel connected.

Realizing what she said before was a little off.

Well, maybe I don't have to join a convent where they don't speak. Maybe that's overreacting. But it is hard to be around civilization. I don't like people. But there are nice people, though, aren't there? Yes. I'm sure you're very nice— although I'm just trying to ingratiate myself to you so you don't try to cut any of my body parts off.

Laughs, then cries.

Now I'm sad.

Suddenly looks up, scared.

Now I'm frightened.

The emotions pass.

No, now I'm fine. Listen to the ocean. That's why I wanted to come on this vacation, and have a summer share at the beach. I wanted to hear the ocean. But you know, I forgot to listen to it the whole time I was with those people. But I'm going to listen to it now.

Listens; she and the the audience hear the sound of the waves; tension leaves Betty's face and body.

Oh, that's lovely. Yes. Ocean, waves, sand. I'm starting to feel better.

Betty smiles at the audience. Closes her eyes. Continues to relax her body.

Sound of the ocean continues.

Lights dim.

End of play.